Slick Move Guide

LATEST EDITION

Be Prepared For Your Journey!

By

Jodi Velazquez

Slick Move, LLC • P.O. Box 243 • Presto, Pennsylvania 15142

Release Date 2014

Printed and Published by Slick Move LLC
P.O. Box 243
Presto, Pennsylvania 15142

Certified Women's Business
Environmentally Friendly Business

Library of Congress Control Number: 2014903993
ISBN: 978-0-615-97541-2

Visit **www.slickmove.net** to read Jodi's blog posts and order her books via Amazon.com.

Disclaimer
Slick Move, LLC cannot accept any responsibility for any injury or damage that you may cause to yourself, others or property when following any advice suggested in the Slick Move Guide. Slick Move, LLC has no control of how you may utilize information in this book. Use advice and information found in the Slick Move Guide at your own risk.

Special Thanks To:

Everyone who has purchased the original Slick Move Guide, the continuous orders have let me know that the information is valuable and helpful. For this reason I have created this new updated version.

To my husband, John, who taught me so much about moving and was the backbone of the original Slick Move Guide.

Melba Cantu – Graphic Artist-Cover Design

Renee Horner – Design and Layout-ThreeEGraphicDesign.com

Kim Conley – Primary Editing

Elayne Masters – Editing

Patricia Martini – Preliminary Editing

Lee Drozak - Web designer-My Office Assistant

Ed Meyers – Print Production Coordinator

South Hills Movers – Cover Endorsement

Contributors: Bill Brack, South Hills Movers, Brianna Hambright, Marcy & Don Madl, Pete & Carol Gorman, Alan Ballo-Scott Township Police, Larry Wildman

Table of Contents

Book Description

The Slick Move Guide Latest Edition is an updated version of the original Slick Move Guide. This consumer written, easy to read, informative and very detailed moving guide that can save a mover hundreds of dollars is now loaded with even more helpful information. Detailed content has been added primarily in the "Determining a good prospect" section to better assist readers with choosing a quality mover and protect them from moving fraud. A comparison of moving yourself and having a moving company relocate your household goods has been added as well as the benefits of moving in the winter months. The original SMG has been tested for competency and changes have been made in determined areas to help the reader understand the information more easily. A section has been added on transporting firearms and more helpful tips have been added about how to handle the emotional side of moving and staying in touch with family and friends. Some editorial revisions have also been made to the new version.

Just as the original this guide offers great packing advice, and will educate the mover on how to protect their household goods, choose a quality mover, and avoid those infamous mistakes and much more. With a spiral binding, it acts as a workbook and the stress reducing timeline in the end of the book is one of the best features providing blank lines for customizing your to do list. It is used by companies, home builders, real estate agents, schools, and sports teams and leagues in America.

Contains Eco-Friendly Moving Advice!

About the Author

Jodi J. Velazquez was born and raised in Pittsburgh, Pennsylvania. Jodi graduated from Robert Morris University with a bachelor degree in marketing communications with an emphasis on writing skills. After graduating, Jodi left Pittsburgh to accompany her husband who accepted a job in Texas with the government. In Texas, Jodi worked for the local paper as a graphic artist and briefly in the editorial department. After two years, her husband received a promotion and the couple moved to New York. There, Jodi worked as an account executive selling television commercial time for a cable company. After three years and the birth of their first child, her husband again accepted another promotion and they left for Philadelphia, Pennsylvania. It was in Philadelphia that their daughter of 19 months was diagnosed with type-one diabetes. This brought a hardship transfer and they moved back to Pittsburgh, Pennsylvania. After their return to Pittsburgh and the birth of their second child, Jodi began writing the Slick Move Guide.

After writing and self-publishing the Slick Move Guide in 2007, she began marketing the book to various organizations and corporations. A major home builder purchased hundreds of copies but the real estate market was declining. She began searching for other industries with a need for the product. The Slick Move Guide to help families that are personally financing their own relocation. She began marketing the book to sports teams for the players and their spouses/partners/families.

One of the teams placed a large order and she realized there was a need. Player development directors liked the idea of a consumer written guide for players who were entering or departing from their team. She established a relationship with several player development directors of major sports teams. They began offering suggestions, mishaps and dilemmas that players encountered, to add to her book. After two years of compiling this information, she released a customized version, Slick Move Guide Professional Athlete edition in 2012.

Although the book was developed with sports professionals it's also of value to anyone who may be making a career transition for the first time or multiple times. One of the differences between the Athlete edition edition and the original Slick Move Guide is that vital inside information that pertains to an athlete's unique situation such as moving quickly and possibly temporarily has been added.

Both guides are easy to read, and offer eco-friendly packing advice and explain how to choose a quality mover. These spiral-bound, lightweight workbooks contain valuable, stress reducing timelines. Jodi has made moving your possessions inexpensive and stress-free!

A portion of the proceeds from this book will be donated to the Juvenile Diabetes Research Foundation in honor of her daughter.

Introduction

My husband and I moved five times in six years. Four of the moves were more than five hours away. Although these moves were to advance my husband's career, *none of them were paid for by his employer*. Three of the moves were in the summer, and two of the moves were in the winter. We made these moves with two pets. On the last two, we also had an infant. *We learned very quickly how to cut costs, pack wisely and quickly, and stay organized.* Our fourth and fifth moves were a breeze because we used Box Number Sheets, and we had become so good at packing and obtaining inexpensive packing supplies.

The Slick Move Guide presents ideas and options to help you make choices about moving to fit your budget and plans. The Slick Move Guide is also designed to inform you of the most difficult and stressful aspects of moving so you can get prepared, be organized, and not be caught off guard. Your move can be stress free!

If you pack your own boxes when you move, you can save 30 to 40 % on the total cost of your move as opposed to having someone pack your belongings. However, there are no guarantees that you will not break something. This guide offers suggestions as well as packing tips and techniques that worked well for us. We never broke an item in all the five times that we moved.

If You Are Considering Moving

Buy a Move Folder and Notebook

The very first thing that you should do is buy a folder and notebook! Today, many of us store information on our phones, laptops and on flash-drives. This is a great way to store information, however, when you move, especially an out of state move, you take a chance of your possessions being separated from you. For this reason, I recommend a moving folder and a hard copy of some of your most important relocation documents.

You will need to investigate a lot to ensure that moving is the right decision. While you are investigating, you can keep all of the information that you gather in this folder. If you decide that you are going to move, this folder will become even more important. Label the folder with the current year and title it "Move Folder." Keep this folder in a place where you keep important items that you use a lot like your purse or wallet. You will appreciate this folder when tax season comes and you want to report all of your expenses for your move.

The folder will be for all the moving receipts, business cards, newspapers, brochures, important papers, information, etc. If you have signed a contract with a moving company to transport your household goods or any contracts related to your move, you should keep the contract in the Move Folder! Your very important inventory list and move "number" assigned to your shipment that the mover gives you should also be kept in your Move Folder so that you have it immediately at your new location. You should keep all receipts of move related items in your move folder. Receipts of everything you buy from mailing tape, motel receipts to truck rentals should go in this folder. These receipts will be needed when you file your income tax if your move is job related; these moving expenses are tax deductible.

It is helpful to put your previous landlord's information (if applicable) in your move folder. Many job and lease applications require this information. If you are waiting for your security-deposit check in the mail and you do not receive it, you will need to contact your previous landlord.

The notebook will be used for all the information that you learn about the new area and any important information about your move. When you travel to a new area to research, you can write down things that you see along the way (names of hotels, motels, post offices, real estate agencies, medical facilities, etc.) You can write important information such as the name, number, and address of all of your current utility companies in the notebook in case you misplace a bill. Keep the notebook inside the move folder. Having this all in one place is a dream come true when you realize that you cannot find a bill that may be packed in a box on the truck. It is so easy to misplace items when you have your house turned upside down because you are moving.

INVESTIGATE - Before You Make a Decision to Move!

Research Your Destination

Some surprises are good, but not all are good! You should research the area where you plan on moving. Sometimes you do not have a choice about where you are moving. However, learning as much as you can prior to moving is wise. Take a week or weekend trip to this area if it is possible. Stay in a motel/hotel and speak to as many people as you can. Tell them that you are planning on moving there and ask them for their opinion of the area. If you are just moving locally, spend some time in the new area and ask people that you meet questions about the area, you will be surprises what you might learn.

One of the most important things that you should buy, once you arrive at the area of interest, is a **MAP!** By looking at a map you can see where very populated and less populated areas are. You can locate, parks, hospitals, and see where the interstates in the area travel, etc. If your GPS or Internet fail, you will still have the map! Pick up newspapers, apartment guides, real estate magazines, and try to get business cards from everywhere that you stop, and keep them in your move folder. Get business cards from real estate agencies, storage centers, employment offices, medical centers, etc. Try to borrow or buy the Yellow Pages phone book for the area you are planning on moving to just in case you lose your internet connection. You can purchase this book through your phone company. Look for a customer service number inside your current Yellow Pages book or online at the directorystore.com. It is also a good idea to take your current Yellow Pages with you when you move.

If your company has given you a promotion and you must move, make sure that the cost of living in the new area does not cancel out your new pay increase. Investigate as much as you can about the cost of living!

Talk To a Real Estate Agent in the Desired Area

Whether you will be renting an apartment or a home or buying a home, it is a good idea to talk with a real estate agent in that area as soon as you can. Some real estate agencies will assist with finding a rental for you if you are not buying. If you do not have a lot of time to apartment hunt, this can be very helpful. Not all areas of the country are the same when it comes to real estate. In some areas it is very easy to rent a house; however, in other areas you may not be able to find a house for rent. It can be very difficult to find an apartment that you like in a big city due to high demand and low supply. My husband and I used to laugh about getting the paper when the ink was still wet and driving to see an apartment with our checkbook in hand only to stand in line behind five other people! Other areas have plenty of nice apartment rentals available all the time.

Be Prepared For Your Journey! • INVESTIGATE - Before You Make a Decision to Move!

7

Some areas may not mind pets while other areas may have strict no-pet policies. Finding a rental when you have an animal may be difficult. A real estate agent will most likely be familiar with which rentals permit animals and which do not.

It is also a good idea to never listen to just one opinion about an area. If someone tells you that an area is too expensive or that it is a bad neighborhood, take a drive and see for yourself! Make sure that you get a lot of opinions.

A real estate agent can also help with:
They are familiar with the area and can help you find the type of neighborhood you desire. They can also tell you about traffic problems in the area. They can help you with your relocation time frame.

A New Residence
Whether you are moving to a home or an apartment, it is important to know the costs. It is important to have a Plan B. If you move to an area and you are unhappy with your place, you may want to move to a nearby neighborhood in a year or so. So, if you can, research a few surrounding towns as well as the one you plan on moving to. Once, after a move, my husband and I were very unhappy in a neighborhood due to crime. In one year, we moved seven miles north to a wonderful town where we felt very safe. If you find an apartment or home and the cost is surprisingly affordable, do not be afraid to ask why. We found a newly built condominium once that was fairly inexpensive for the size. After signing the lease, we discovered that it was five minutes from a nuclear power plant. Look around! Just ask the real estate agent or landlord why a place is so inexpensive or so expensive. What does the place offer for that price? Inquire about what the pros and cons of the neighborhood are.

Sometimes you may feel rushed when looking at an apartment or a home. Take your time; it is a big decision. Open cabinets and closets, inspect walls, look at bathrooms for water damage or mold, inspect all appliances, and ask if anything is broken or not working correctly. If the place you are looking at has a fireplace, ask if it is working properly and if it is vented properly. Do not forget to ask if you will get your security deposit back if you move again. If your job is not permanent, ask if you can have a flexible lease.

Also, look to see if the place will be easy to move into or out of. Is there a driveway or enough room for a truck? Will any neighbors' cars be parked in front of the place when you need to get the moving truck close to the door? If you are renting an apartment, it is a good idea to get the landlords cell phone number so you can call him or her the day of the move if you need a neighbor's car moved or if you have any problems. If you move to a place where it is not easy for a moving truck to get close to your front door, you could be charged an extra fee by the moving company for a long-carry.

If you plan on putting in a pool, make sure there is not any rock or clay on the property. Make sure there are not any ordinances prohibiting pools. How much shade will the potential pool area receive? Will trees have to be removed?

If there are a lot of major corporations in an area, there will most likely be a lot of "transient" residents (people who are not originally from the area). If there are not a lot of major corporations, the area may have a lot of residents who have lived there all of their lives. In my opinion, a transient area tends to be easier to find a home, meet neighbors, and make friends.

Insurance

Car insurance is another important part of your financial puzzle. Your existing car insurance policy will have to be transferred to a new policy. If you are leaving a small town and moving to a larger city, your car insurance most likely will go up. This is a part of the "cost of living" that can sometimes be overlooked because it may not be paid monthly. It is important to find out if your car insurance and homeowners/renters insurance will cost more in the area that you want to move to. You will need a residence to get new insurance in your new area. However, you can most likely get an idea of what insurance will cost if you can provide them with a possible address. You could use the address/zip code of your new place of employment just to get an idea of what the new insurance may cost. Speak to your insurance agent or ask for a free quote, which most major insurance companies now offer on their websites. It is much easier to open a new policy in a new state if you have been with a national company for some time because of your established history as a good customer. If your car insurance and homeowners/renters insurance are with a national insurance company, the transition should be fairly easy. In fact, you should not lose any of your credits/discounts that you may have accumulated through your car insurance over the years.

If you are selling a home, and you need to move before it sells, call your insurance agent to inquire about "specific language" in your homeowner's policy that may prohibit you from leaving your home vacant.

If you are buying a home, here are a few factors that affect the cost of homeowners insurance:

- Age of the house

- Type of construction

- If it has a security system

- Proximity to a fire hydrant (If outside of 1,000 feet, you may pay a premium.)

- If it is in an urban or rural market

- Proximity to a coastal shoreline

When purchasing a home ALWAYS hire a professional inspector to inspect the home before you purchase.

You will want to know exactly what to expect, indoors and out, in terms of costs for repair and maintenance. A fresh coat of paint could be hiding serious structural problems or watermarks in the basement may indicate a chronic seepage problem. The home inspector interprets these and other clues, and then presents his professional opinion as to the condition of the property before you buy it, so you can avoid unpleasant and possibly costly surprises afterwards.

Utilities

It is very important to research utility companies in your new area prior to moving there. Find out if you will have propane, gas, forced air, electric heat, oil fire furnace, coal furnace, or hot water heat. You can call your future utility company and ask them what the average monthly costs are in the area. Again, you may need an address or zip code to obtain this information. Ask what additional start up fees or costs there are. My husband and I were caught very off guard once by a large mandatory deposit just to get our gas turned on. We had just paid a large mandatory first month's rent and security deposit, and we were not prepared for the large gas deposit!

Once, we did not have our garbage picked up for three weeks after moving into an apartment. I learned that we needed to call the disposal company and place an order to have our garbage picked up. We also learned that if it was not in specific garbage cans, it would not be picked up, and boxes had to be broken down and bound with string! Ask a lot of questions when you call utility and service organizations. Most utilities are paid monthly, and for this reason, this is an area of extreme concern. You definitely do not want any surprises in with your utilities. Utilities are part of your monthly financial puzzle, and they absolutely need to fit. Research and be sure you know the costs!

New Healthcare

Investigate what options you will have for new healthcare in the area where you are planning on moving. Your current healthcare provider may not be available in the new area. For instance, this area may offer only HMOs.

Important Places to Locate

Look for hospitals, medical centers, veterinarian clinics, post offices, laundromats, etc., in the new area. Write down the names and try to get business cards from these places to keep in your move folder. Investigate to see if the hospitals and medical centers are reputable.

Locate hotels and motels around the area in case there is a delay with your moving into your new residence. There are long-term-lease/extended-stay hotels that have kitchens and laundry appliances. Look for restaurants and pizza shops, and collect business cards! You may want to order a pizza after unloading and unpacking! Consider being close to the airport if you plan on traveling a lot.

Chamber of Commerce Help

An essential number to have in your move folder is the local Chamber of Commerce in your new area. The people who work at the chambers are very willing to help you obtain information on organizations, entertainment, schools, demographics, census tables, and places of worship. They can inform you about websites to help you learn about the area, and some chambers will send you a welcome kit. If the chamber can provide cost of living information about the town that you are moving to, you can compare it to websites that offer cost of living information about the town. If they do not provide the information you need, they may be able to get it for you or provide phone numbers where you can obtain it.

Shopping

Find out how many malls are in the area and what kind of stores are in them. Are they mostly top designer stores? Are there any moderately priced department stores? Are there any dollar stores in the area? It may be hard to imagine, but there are areas that are saturated with expensive stores but have a shortage of inexpensive stores and vice versa. Finding an area that has both is ideal. Research the restaurants in the area as well. If fast food is part of your daily or weekly routine, see if your favorite stops are in the new area. Not all areas have cheap fast food! My husband and I discovered once after moving that the only quick bites to eat for breakfast were delicatessens at the tune of $8 to $10 for a sandwich and coffee! (1990's) Also, find out what the sales tax is. This should be on all of your receipts from purchases in the area. Do not just rely on one website to give you the cost of living in a particular area. Collect newspapers, local papers, and magazines to research costs of groceries, restaurants, cars, etc.

Traffic

Spending a week in the area that you would like to move to before making a firm decision is very wise. Traffic is an important factor. The traffic in the new area could be a lot more congested than you are used to. How much time will this add to your morning and evening commute? Is the traffic so congested that you will avoid driving to your favorite stores? Will you be happy with the stores that are closest to you? Are these stores in your price range? How much will your fuel costs increase? Being close to hotels, a school, and public transportation can all be very important factors in making your daily life comfortable.

Neighborhoods

Learn about the neighborhood before you move there. My best advice for this is talking to the people who live there and driving around an area. When moving to a new area, it is important to research the crime statistics in several ways, as it is not always accurate. Look for things that may give clues, like references to "gated community." A lot of gated communities are gated just for privacy; however, some are gated to protect the community inside. If you are in an urban area at night and the traffic lights at intersections are blinking red lights, you may want to talk to the local police and ask why. If crime is high in an area, they may not want people sitting in their car at a traffic light at night so the light blinks red so you can stop and quickly go. We moved to an area once that appeared to be nice; however, there was a huge problem with auto theft. Be observant and ask questions! Do not be afraid to contact the local police in the area and ask questions. Drive through the area at night as well as during the day. Installing a security system when you move to a new area is a great idea.

Education

You can investigate the schools in the area if you have children. **Schoolmatch.com, Greatschools.net** and **PSK12.com** (public school ranking) are websites that offer school-performance information on elementary, middle, and high schools for most states. Will the school be able to accommodate your child's interests? Ask if the school has a nurse (not all do). It is nice to live close to a school because this cuts down on travel time if you have to make trips to the school. See what kinds of private schools and colleges are in the area. A real estate agent may be able to help with some of your questions about schools. They may be able to recommend a school that has exactly what you are looking for.

Taxes

Another very important fact to research is taxes in the area. The Chamber of Commerce should be able to supply state, retail, city, and real estate tax information on their area as well as surrounding areas, which may be quite different. There are usually county websites that give real estate tax information on certain properties. Real estate agents can help with this as well.

Talk to all types of workers in the area, like waitresses, gas station attendants, car salesman, business owners, and doctors. These people may fill you in on hidden secrets of the area. For example, my husband and I moved to an area that was fairly destitute and bragged about having no state tax. However, because it was so destitute, there were incredible shipping taxes on every kind of product coming in. This canceled out the "no state tax" feature. Some states that have "no state tax" impose a "value tax."

If you are building a home or buying a home in an undeveloped area, it is important to note that the taxes may rise several years after you move in to accommodate the area's growth and needs.

Also, when purchasing a house, your taxes may be based on the sale price that you pay and not the property value that was placed on the house previously.

Income

If you are moving because of your partner's job, you may not research much about what kind of salary you will make in the new area. Do not assume that the area pays the same salary/wages as your current area because salaries and wages fluctuate throughout the United States. If you work in city limits, you will pay a city wage tax. Find out what this tax will be.

Transportation

Research the options available for public transportation in the area you are moving. We moved to a small town on the outskirts of a big city once and were surprised to find out that it was one of the only surrounding towns that did not provide public transportation. Some exclusive small communities do not want public transportation. The chamber of commerce in the area should be able to help you with this. They can provide detailed local, city, and state maps.

When You Have Decided That You Are Going to Move

Putting in a Request to Have Your Utilities Turned Off/On

You can call a utility company to turn services on or off or you can do this on-line. In either case getting a confirmation number and/or receipt is vital! Utility companies can be called a month or two before you move, and you can put an order in for your power, gas, water, cable, etc., to be shut off the day after you move. I do not recommend having any important utilities shut off the day that you are moving. Make sure that you stress this to the person who handles your request. Cell phones have made it a little easier if your phone actually gets shut off the morning of your move. However, you do not want your electricity or water turned off the morning of the move, so emphasize the importance of the date when requesting that your utilities be terminated. You may have to charge your cell phone and you will need electricity on! I highly recommend scheduling a couple of hours one day during a work week prior to moving to call all of your utility companies and creditors. Scheduling shutting off utilities, providing dates and changing your address, may take some time so prepare for this.

When you call your utility companies to request that your service be shut off, remember to get the name of the person that you spoke to. Write this name in your move folder. Most companies provide a confirmation number for your order, which you should also write in your move notebook next to the representative's name. If you are doing this online, print this information. This is important because if, for some reason, your utilities are not shut off and you receive a bill at your new residence for services past the date that you ordered them to be shut off, you can quickly provide them with the name of the person you spoke to and the confirmation number. With this information, you will not be responsible for services past the turn-off date. You can put a statement from each utility company in your move folder for a quick reference on account numbers.

It is also very important to make sure that your current utility companies are paid in full. They do not usually send a bill for unpaid services when you leave their region and may simply turn you into a collection agency. It is ideal if you know your new address before you request shut off so you can give this to them in case of any problems with your account. If you do not know your new address, consider getting a post-office box in your new town or using your new employer's address.

Other services that you will have to cancel might include cable television, newspaper, security, pest control, lawn maintenance, and cleaning help.

You will also need to have the utilities turned on at your new residence on the day that you move, and you should keep the names and addresses of your new utility companies in your move folder just in case the utilities are not turned on. All service-connection confirmation numbers should be in the move folder as well.

There are companies on-line that connect utilities for people that are moving. Some of them offer rate comparing, selecting new utilities, disconnecting the old utilities and setting up the new utilities with ease. Although I have never used a service like this, it is worth investigating.

Notification of Change of Address

For some reason, changing your address over the phone does not always work. Some companies have a "change of address" box you can check on your statement. I found this to work very well. Most credit card websites will allow you to change your address online if you are set up to make your payment online. I recommend www.USPS.com. Avoiding changing your address can cause problems if utilities or any debts are not paid in full.

Setting a Move Date

You may not have a choice about the date that you have to relocate. Summer moves are nice for Northerners because you avoid moving in the cold weather and possibly snow; however, you may have to move in the rain. If you are moving out of state, transport rates are usually higher in the summer. Winter moves can be a challenge because of weather, but you will have less expensive transport costs for an out-of-state move. As soon as you set a date, you should immediately call a few moving companies to come and give you an estimate. In order to get the date that you want, you have to give the moving companies at least two months notice. By planning ahead, you can secure the date that you need. Many people who are renting or selling a house need to be out by a certain date, so getting the move date set in stone with a moving company is very important. One of the most difficult and stressful aspects of moving is to coordinate your termination of your current residence, your moving truck arriving at the proper time, and moving into your new residence on time. You must have good communication, and really stress to landlords and rental people that firm dates are necessary. When you are buying or selling a house, it can be very hard to coordinate around a closing date. You may have to stay with friends or in an extended-stay motel if you cannot get into your new residence when you need to. **When setting your move date keep in mind that rates for moving companies and renting trucks are usually lower mid-month, mid-week, and during the fall and winter months.**

Moving Services

Making a decision about how you are going to move your household goods can be compared to going out to dinner! You can go to a restaurant and sit down and have your dinner served to you, you may order dinner but go to the salad bar, you could choose a buffet or go to a drive-through. Often, your budget helps you determine your dinner plans. Just like going out to dinner, there are many options available for transporting your household goods.

Factors That Will Help You Determine How You Will Move

What is your moving budget? If your company is handling the relocation costs, find out exactly what is covered and what you are responsible for.

- How much do you have to move?

- How far are you moving?

- When are you moving?

- Do you have help?

- Will you be using a storage unit?

Determining a Good Prospect

Check Credentials

Before you decide on a company, you should do a background check on that company by calling the Better Business Bureau or going online at **BBB.org.** Make sure that the mover is <u>registered</u> with the **Federal Motor Carrier Safety Administration (FMCSA)** and they have a **United States Department of Transportation (USDOT)** number. You can determine if a mover is registered with FMCSA by accessing the website **www.protectyourmove.gov.** On this website you can learn a tremendous amount about the legalities of moving and transporting goods. It is important to note that each state varies with rules and regulations for the transportation industry within its state. If you are moving out of state, the moving company that you choose should have an **Interstate Commerce Commission (ICC MC)** number. They should also have a **Public Utility Commission (PUC)** number, if not; they may be regulated by a government entity. A reputable moving company should provide you with the booklet *Your Rights and Responsibilities When You Move or legal disclosure forms,* provided by the U.S. Department of Transportation. Make the time to read the booklet to learn about the company's regulations, policies, dispute-settlement policies, damaged-goods policies, and insurance options for your shipment. Prior to moving, the moving company is required to provide you with a copy of their dispute-settlement-program information. Learning and understanding all of this information can be overwhelming, but it is necessary in order to protect your household goods.

How Will the Cost Be Determined?

Some moving companies charge by an hourly rate, and some charge by weight and mileage. Do they have a minimum charge? How will you be charged after the minimum is met? What is included, and what do they charge extra for? Is there an extra cost for stairs (flight charge) or the disassembly of beds, electronics, and/or appliances? Do they charge for the travel time between their office and your home? Is there a different rate for weekends and/or nights?

Get an Estimate

Once your budget is determined, and you know what you can afford to spend. Then you can start getting estimates to determine your move method. The rule of thumb is to get at least three estimates from companies, whether you are using a full-service professional moving company or renting a truck to do it yourself. Reputable moving companies offer free, no-obligation estimates. It is important to know whether the estimate (all the charges for services the mover will perform) that you get is *binding or nonbinding*. A binding estimate is a fixed price in writing. A nonbinding estimate is a price that will be determined after the moving truck goes through a weigh station with your shipment before arriving at the final destination. If it is non-binding and the actual weight of your shipment determined at the weigh station is more than expected, you will be responsible for paying up to 10 percent of the "over" amount at the time of delivery. You will be responsible for the remainder. Some states allow only nonbinding estimates.

25 Areas for Questioning a Moving Company

1. Will a representative come to your home and give you a no-obligation, free estimate? Over the phone estimates are just a guess and never accept an verbal estimate.

2. How will cost be determined? By the hour, the weight of the shipment, mileage? If by weight, how will this be determined?

3. Do they have a minimum charge, and how are you charged after the minimum is met? Do they charge in fifteen-minute or half-hour increments?

4. Will there be any unforeseen costs? Will they be able to move all of your items? Will there be an extra cost for very large items? Are there additional costs for disassembling or reassembling furniture? Will they cover your mattresses?

5. Can you save money by disassembling and reassembling the beds/furniture yourself, having all the items on the first floor, and/or crating items yourself?

6. Are there any other ways to save money on the move?

7. Will there be a travel charge/service charge? Movers who do not impose a travel charge may have a higher hourly rate. Is there an extra charge for evenings/weekends?

8. Ask if the moving company is a broker, or if they have their own equipment to transport your shipment. Do they use subcontractors?

9. What kind of cancellation policy do they offer? (You should be able to cancel or postpone your move up until a few days before your move date.)

10. Do they employ temps or day-labor employees? An employee working full time for a company may have more experience. What kind of training have their movers completed?

11. What type of insurance (cargo protection, valuation protection) do they offer? (This should be posted on the bill of laden.) Even if a moving company is bonded and insured, that does not mean that your items are covered during the move. Some states require that a company put a valuation of 60 cents per pound coverage on a shipment. This may not be enough and may include and exclude items and events. For example, a leather purse may only weigh two pounds and Acts of nature such as floods may prevent reimbursement. Your homeowners or a third party insurance company can be an alternative.

12. What forms of payment do they accept: cash, check, credit, cashier's check, or traveler's checks? (Be cautious of a company that only accepts cash or does not accept cash.)

---

13. What types of payment options do they offer? Is a deposit required? Will you pay half before and the balance at drop off?

14. If you are moving within your state, ask the driver if he will have to cross the state lines at some point, which will turn your move into an interstate move.

15. Will your estimate be binding or nonbinding?

16. Can they give you an exact time for pick-up and for delivery?

17. What is the longest that their "drop-off window" (time when your household items are in transport) could be? Will the pick up and drop-off dates be written on the contract?

18. You should ask about the order in which your shipment will be picked up. Will your order be picked up first and dropped off last or picked up last and dropped off first? Ask how many other customers' household goods will be on the truck with yours.

19. Will they provide an inventory sheet?

20. Will there be a way for you to contact the driver after pick-up and before drop-off in case any problems occur?

21. What is the policy for lost and damaged items? Make sure the company has an arbitration program for resolving any disputes concerning damage or loss to your shipment.

22. If you are not at the destination when the movers arrive, will your shipment go into a storage facility?

23. Do the movers use storage facilities with climate control?

24. If an item is lost, will they contact the other clients whose household goods were on the truck with yours to see if they accidentally received your item?

25. What are your rights and responsibilities on moving day?

What Moving Options Are Available

A full service professional move will most likely be the most expensive way to move, although it is the easiest. You will hire a full-service moving company, and they will come to your current home and pack your household goods, load them onto their truck, and then transport them to your new residence where they will unload your shipment. Full-service moving companies can move you locally, intrastate (within the state), or interstate (out of state). In our experience, we found that our interstate moves were the least expensive because discounts were offered for the amount of household goods that we had and because we moved during the non-peak season (winter months). The move season is typically April through September, and during this time the costs are generally higher. The most expensive move for us was an "intra move" which is moving within the same state. In the particular state that we were in, the Public Utility Commission regulated the intra moves, and no discounts were available. So for us, the most expensive move that we made was the one where we moved the least distance.

Customizing a Full-Service Professional Move

There are many ways that you can customize and save money with a professional moving company.

- You can pack your household goods by yourself and then have a moving company load and transport them to your new residence.

- You can pack your own household goods, rent a moving truck, and hire a moving company to come to your home and load the packed boxes onto the truck that you rented. If the moving company has a franchise at your destination, you can even have the same moving company unload your items.

- You can hire a moving company to move only the very large items in your home such as sofas, entertainment centers, beds, chests of drawers, tables, etc. Then you can rent a truck and transport the other items.

- Avoiding steps: There will most likely be an extra charge to remove items from the upstairs of your home and to deliver certain items upstairs in your new residence. This is called a "flight charge." At the origination point, you can have all of your household goods on the first floor to avoid an extra charge for the movers to go upstairs. At the destination, you can have the movers unload only on the first floor of your new residence and move items to the upstairs yourself.

- You can wrap your own mattresses and furniture with stretch wrap.

- You can disassemble all of your furniture, appliances, and electronics.

- You can reassemble all of your furniture, appliances, and electronics.

- You can crate your mirrors and glass items.

- Some moving companies include setting up beds in the cost of the move; others will charge you extra. Make sure that you know the cost and decide who will be responsible for this service.

Get It in Writing!

Once you have decided on a moving company, you will want to make sure that important issues (how you have customized your move) are written on the estimate. For example, if the movers will be stopping at a storage facility for you, if you are paying extra to have specialty items packed such as pool tables or a grandfather clock, or if you are moving all of your household goods to the first floor to save money. Read the estimate and bill of lading (receipt for your goods and contract for their transportation). Make sure everything you agreed upon is included and stated correctly. You should be given a partially completed copy of the bill of lading prior to the carrier departing with your household goods.

Know the Length of Your Drop-Off Window

Lastly, make sure the estimate is signed by the mover. The mover should also provide you with an order for service, a list detailing all the services the mover will perform on the agreed-upon dates. Make sure that the dates work for you and are correct. This document is very important and should be reviewed and agreed upon by both parties. Your shipment will most likely be consolidated with other shipments on the truck. The movers may unload in reverse order to protect your belongings. In other words, if your shipment is the last to be loaded on the truck, it will be the first to be delivered. This is ideal because it gives you the shortest "drop-off window" (time when your household items are in transport). During the drop-off window, you will be without your household goods, and you must be available at your new residence during this time in case your delivery arrives. It is good to ask as many questions as you can about the drop-off window. You may have to dine out during this time, so factor that into your budget.

Carefully read the information on the bill of lading, order for service, estimate, and any other documents before you sign them. Make sure that everything that you talked about and agreed upon is noted and correct. After your items are loaded, make sure that you receive a copy of the inventory list showing each item you are shipping and its condition. Check this list and make sure that it is correct. Do not sign blank documents under any circumstances! You can determine if a mover has assessed the correct transportation charges for your shipment by calling the **Surface Transportation Board at (866) 254-1792.**

A Few Options to Avoid

- Never get an estimate over the phone because this would be just a guess.

- Be cautious of hiring a mover over the Internet and sending money without checking credentials.

- Inexpensive can be dangerous. Remember, when shipping your household goods, do not look for the least expensive option. Go with reputable! A second-rate company that you find on the Internet may contract your job out to another company who you never heard of or researched! A second-rate company could cancel at the last minute. Their trucks may be very old and unreliable.

Self-Service Movers

A self-service move is when a company drops off a crate or trailer and you pack your household goods. Then you load your goods into their truck and drive to your new home. The customer can use as much of the trailer as they need. Price is computed by linear feet used and how far your shipment will go. If you are able to pack yourself and you are confident that you can load a moving truck properly, this option may be beneficial to you. However, you should compare estimates to see if you will save money by using a self-service moving company as opposed to packing yourself and using a full-service professional moving company to transport your household goods. Self-service moving companies sometimes only accommodate an out-of-state move.

Renting a Moving Truck

If you decide that you are going to move your household items/boxes yourself, you have chosen the way that requires the most work for you! However, you have most likely chosen the least expensive way to move, but you will need a lot of help! Having eight to ten friends who can help is ideal. When you rent a truck, you are on a time schedule and the more helpers you have, the easier it is to load and unload quickly. Staying organized is important when loading and unloading, and you do not want the added pressure of having to rush. You do not want to exceed your time or mileage "limits" when you rent a truck. Unloading is just as important as loading. It can be a real nightmare if your kitchen items are buried in the garage because you were in a hurry to return the truck.

You will need to research and shop around for the best prices on renting a truck. The truck rental company can help you determine the appropriate size truck for the move by the number of rooms and the square footage of your residence. You should have those measurements and information written down. If you are moving close by and are considering renting a smaller truck and making two trips to save money, be aware that when you rent a truck, you also incur the fees/costs of gas, mileage, and time when you return the truck later than your agreement states. It may actually be less expensive to rent a larger truck and make only one trip. You will also work much harder making several trips.

The "Smart Packing" section explains how you can limit your number of boxes by using items you have as packing materials, putting items inside each other, and filling boxes appropriately without making the boxes too heavy. Packing this way will give you less boxes to move! The "Smart Packing" and "Moving Day" sections will also give you tips on how to organize your boxes/household goods so that on moving day you are ready to pack the truck and you can unpack quickly at the destination, staying organized the whole time. Time is money when you are renting a moving truck!

Research the cost of renting a truck for "one way" and compare it to renting the truck and returning it to the place of origination (round trip). Driving the empty truck back may take time but it may save you a lot of money and you may have to return to your former home anyway. The cost of fuel will have to be considered. The majority of rental trucks are 26 feet in length and get six to eight miles per gallon of gas.

If you are renting a truck, you are most likely doing all the loading and unloading as well. Most truck rental companies also rent hand trucks/utility dollies. They are inexpensive to rent and can cut your loading and unloading time in half. You can rent two or three if you have a lot of helpers. Most utility dollies/hand trucks have load-locking straps and stair climbers that help make moving bulky refrigerators, stoves, washers and dryers much easier. There are three types of dollies:

- **Utility dolly/hand truck.** This dolly stands upright with two wheels and a "scoop" for sliding under stoves, dryers, boxes, and dressers. The items can then be transported with ease. Folding hand trucks/utility dollies are also available.

- **Appliance dolly/hand truck.** This dolly is taller and can handle heavier appliances such as refrigerators, freezers, and washers.

- **Furniture dolly.** This dolly is four-wheeled with a flat surface and is used to move large dressers, freezers, pianos/organs, and wall units.

You can also rent **furniture pads** which can really make a difference in protecting your furniture!

Before you sign a contract with a truck rental company, you should read the entire contract and ask if there are any extra costs that are not listed. Inquire if the vehicle will have an emergency kit onboard and what kind of shocks the truck will have. Find out if you can return the truck after hours and if so, where you should leave the key. When you go to pick up the truck you have rented, you will want to inspect the truck before you drive it off the lot. Check the oil, fuel, transmission fluid, tires, lights, hazard lights, and radiator before you drive it off the lot. Also check for damage. Compare the fuel-tank gauge and mileage to what is printed on your contract, and make sure they agree.

It is important to have a guarantee that the size truck you need will be available on the day that you want to move. Some truck rental companies rent the same truck several times on Friday or Saturday, and they are usually very busy at the end of the month. If the truck is not returned on time by the person who rents it before you, you may not get the specific size truck that you need. You may get a truck that is smaller or larger. You can increase your chances of getting the truck that you need by moving Sunday through Thursday when the rental companies are less busy. You may be able to get a longer rental time. You may find that the largest truck that you can get is 28 feet, which is supposed to be able to move a four-bedroom house. Some people have more collectibles than others. If you are a collector, have an alternative plan if the 28-foot truck is too small. For example, you may have to make two trips, or downsizing may be another option.

It is also a good idea to purchase a protection plan when you rent a truck in case you get into an accident. You are responsible for any collision damage to the truck unless you have an insurance policy to cover you. Your auto insurance may not cover collision damage to rental trucks. Most major insurance companies will cover you if you rent a car, but they do not cover a vehicle over 10,000 gross vehicle weight (GVW). Even if they do cover you, there may be a deductible and increased premiums. You can buy insurance through the rental company. However, you should research several companies' insurance policies and talk to your insurance agent to compare. Most truck rental companies usually offer insurance for your stored possessions. Many storage customers are in the process of moving between homes and, therefore, may not have homeowner's or renter's insurance policies to protect their goods. Even if they do, the policy may restrict the amount of coverage provided for goods stored away from a customer's residence. If your household goods are going to be in storage for a while, you should investigate the different policy options available and weigh the differences. Rental companies also offer policies to protect those who may be towing their car on a rented auto transport, tow dolly or tow bar, or trailer.

Renting car-top carriers and pulling trailers is a good idea for last minute items and can make leaving a little less stressful. Leaving items behind because you didn't have enough room could be upsetting.

Combination Truck Rental and Moving Company

You can hire a moving company to load and transport only your very large items. For example, a company can come in and give you an estimate to take your beds, dressers and chests, desks, couches, loveseats and recliners, pool tables, dining room table and chairs and any other very large items. Then you can rent a truck and move all of the smaller items yourself. This may be a good idea for a few reasons:

1. You may be limited with help or you have help that is older or may not be able to lift heavy items.

2. You may be worried that the people helping could possibly drop heavy furniture.

3. You may be concerned about someone getting hurt while they are helping you lift heavy furniture.

4. A combination move is convenient for people who own an outdoor tool/lawn equipment shed. If you are moving the outdoor items yourself, you will not have to worry about boxing the items such as tool boxes, buckets, clippers, shovels, lawn chairs, etc. You can put them on the rental truck last and unload them into your new garage or shed first. If these items were going on a moving truck with movers, you would have to box or wrap them to avoid losing them. By transporting these items yourself, you save the time of boxing them, you save money on purchasing the boxes, and you eliminate the worry of losing wrapped or bundled items on a moving truck that you are not driving/following.

If you decide to rent a truck and hire a company, you will need to get all costs on paper and make sure that it will be less expensive for you to do it this way. See what the cost would be for a company to move all of your items, and make sure that you are saving money with a combination move. You will have to decide if you should get the rental truck and move the small items before or after the movers take the big items. The cost of the rental truck will fluctuate, and you may make your choice based on which day will be less expensive.

Storage Unit

It is ideal if you are moving to a place that has the same amount of storage space as your prior residence. However, if you are losing storage space, you may want to consider renting a storage unit. Storage units can also be a benefit financially. Once we moved to a very small apartment and we knew that we would only be there temporarily. We rented a storage unit for three years. The cost of a storage unit every month was far less than what we would have paid monthly for a larger apartment. You may want to keep a portion of your household goods in a storage facility while you look for a home, do some remodeling on your new home, or just get organized.

If you are moving in the winter, it could be raining or snowing on moving day. This could make it difficult to unload items into an outdoor shed or patio. The movers will be walking through your new house a lot, and if the weather is bad, the less they have to bring in, the better. It is nice to just unload all of the outdoor items, holiday items, and/or out-of-season boxes into a nearby storage unit rather than trying to get an outdoor shed or a second garage set up in the midst of getting your new home organized.

Once you are organized and settled in your new home, you can return to the storage unit when the weather is warm and dry and bring the items to your new home at your leisure. It is nice not to have to deal with summer items in the winter and vice versa. Outdoor furniture, lawn equipment, pool supplies, gardening tools, summer clothes, and summer toys can all be marked "storage" and loaded on the truck last. Whether you are driving the truck yourself or if movers are transporting your items, arrange for your storage items to be unloaded at the storage facility before going to your new residence.

If you are using a storage unit, list all items that are inside the box on the outside of the box in black marker so that you can easily read it. If you have the items listed on a sheet of paper, you may loose the paper in six months time. For boxes in storage, I do recommend everything inside be listed on the box with marker. When you return to the storage unit, you will know exactly where the items that you need are. Other items that you may want to designate for the storage unit include attic items, sports equipment, unused electronics and appliances, extra furniture or beds. The Smart Packing section will emphasize how to pack items for storage to avoid damage and smell.

If you are going to use a storage unit, you should try to get one that is relatively close to your new home and one that has "climate control." Outdoor storage units can be hard on electronics/appliances with extreme heat and humidity or cold. Indoor storage facilities can be more expensive but are better for electronics and appliances. Warehouses may or may not have climate control. Ask if they ever had any leakage problems, and if that happens, what is their policy to compensate for your items. Ask if they offer insurance that you can buy to protect your belongings. Ask if the monthly cost will ever be raised or if you are "locked in" and for how long. Some truck rental companies offer one month of free storage as a courtesy.

Unexpected Storage

There is a chance that you may not be able to find an apartment or a house by the time that you need to move. If you are buying, you may not be able to get into your new home when you need to be. Your household goods may have to go into storage. Make sure that you choose a quality storage facility with climate control! Read above.

PODS

Portable on demand storage (PODS) are weather-resistant containers that can withstand 110 mph winds when partially filled. They can be dropped off at your residence so you can pack and load at your leisure. They are rented monthly starting the day they are dropped off. There is a drop-off fee and a reoccurring rental fee if you pass one month's time. Quotes do not include tax and future container pickup and delivery charges. The PODS company does not prorate monthly rates for unused days. Once you are packed, PODS will deliver the container to your new residence. Availability of delivery vehicles and distance to your new location determines how long it will take to deliver. You do not need to be at your new residence when your container is delivered. Large homes may need multiple containers. Costs for PODS are based on the season, delivery charges, transportation charges, and the different franchise charges. PODS quotes are valid for five days.

PODS are a good idea if you are going to have time between moving out of your old residence and moving into your new residence and you do not want to put your household items into a storage facility. PODS are convenient if you are selling and showing your home and want to remove some of the clutter so potential buyers can focus on your home, not what you have in it. Since the PODS unit is delivered for you, this option eliminates you having to drive a moving truck. If you have not found an ideal new residence and are still looking, PODS containers are a nice choice for a temporary move. Your unit will be held in storage and delivered when you find a more permanent residence. This will save you from having to rent and load a truck, unload your household goods into storage, and then rent another truck and load and unload your possessions again.

Research for any changes and read before you sign any contracts when renting moving equipment.

Not Sure What to Do?

Here are some key points in moving yourself and hiring a moving company to transport your household items:

Quality of Trucks

Moving yourself - If you are planning on moving yourself, there are most likely several truck rental companies right in your hometown and you can actually go there and see the trucks that they have available for rent. You have most likely seen them before, either driven by truck rental centers or friends may be able to provide some insight. **If you have done your research on these companies and you have visited their centers then you will most likely have a good idea of the quality of the truck you will be renting.**

Hiring movers - If you choose to hire a moving company there may be some uncertainty as to what kind of truck your household goods will be transported in on moving day. If you have made all of the arrangements online (not recommended) this could really make you uncomfortable and uncertain about the authenticity and quality of the trucks and drivers that will arrive. Therefore, moving yourself does offer a degree of certainty about quality because you most likely know the driver and you have inspected the trucks.

Timing

Moving yourself - Your household good will be with you. You will know where your items are at all times and you are able to retrieve something if you really need to.

Hiring movers - even if you know exactly what your window is (the time frame that the movers have to deliver your items) there can still be a sense of uncertainty. This feeling can make you uncomfortable if you are really relying on receiving your goods quickly. The movers may tell you that your time frame is 3 to 15 days and they may assure you that it "should be" closer to 3 days than 15 but you really can't be sure how it will go.

Security and Trust

Moving yourself - Do you think the chances for lost, stolen or damaged items are less if you move yourself? Yes. You may damage items unintentionally if you move yourself; however, your chances of having items stolen from you are reduced drastically. Items that you believe you lost you will most likely locate after unpacking.

Hiring movers - Hopefully, if you are paying for a full service move, you have thoroughly researched the company that you plan to use and your items will be in good hands. Is there a 100 percent guarantee that all will go well and none of your items will become lost, stolen or damaged? – No.

Cost

Moving yourself - You can save 30 to 40% off the total cost of moving if you pack your household goods yourself. You can most likely save even more if you rent a truck and transport your own household goods.

Hiring movers - Paying for a full service move (having movers come to your home and pack your household goods, load them onto a truck, transport them and then unload them) is the most expensive way to move.

Work and Effort

Moving yourself - You will have to work if you pack your household goods. If you are also transporting them, you may have a lot of work depending on how much help you have.

Hiring movers - For a full service move, you will not have a lot of work. If you are just packing your own household goods, you can rest once the movers take your shipment and you will work again if you are unloading

Whether you move yourself or hire a moving company you will still have some tasks ahead of you. You have to learn where new stores are and find new doctors. You will most likely have a different design for your home and may have to rearrange furniture. Your new home may need some repairs. Adjusting to a new job can be tiring. You will have to meet new people, develop some new friendships and spend some time on the internet changing your address with friends, families and businesses.

Not Sure When? Winter Move vs. Summer Move

Low Rates and Better Availability Can Outweigh the Inconveniences of Moving in the Winter. There are several advantages to relocating in October through March if you are properly prepared for a winter move. The peak moving season is April through September. Prices and rates are higher during this busy season which means they are lower during the winter months - **allowing you to save money!** During the busy moving season availability of trucks, vans, movers, supplies and open dates for when you need to move can be limited due to the high demand. One of the trickiest aspects of moving is being able to move out of your current residence when you need to and move into your new residence when it is available. When the demand is high in the summer months it may be difficult to have the movers arrive when you need them to be there. **The winter months offer less stress with your coordination needs.** If you are renting a moving truck, you will most likely have a better chance of getting the size truck you want as well. Also, during these busy months, moving companies may hire extra help such as students who may be inexperienced. **In the winter you are more likely to have the professional experienced movers handling your shipment. So if you are a person who likes to avoid stress and save money a winter move may be for you.** However, there are several inconveniences that go along with moving in the winter. Being properly prepared is a key to a successful winter move. Here are a few tips:

1. **Realize that the weather could be uncooperative on moving day and be prepared for it.** Acquire a membership to a roadside assistance program and have their number with you. Have your travel route well planned. Locate hotels along the way in case the weather is too bad to continue. Decide way in advance who will be driving vehicles and rental trucks on moving day. Be sure that they can drive in poor weather conditions. In advance, ask your landlord, real estate agent and moving company if you can have a couple extra days to move in and out if the weather is inclement. Choose a friend or relative to stay connected with during your travel so someone knows where you are at all times.

2. **Have all vehicles that are traveling with the move winterized (winter tires, non-freezing washer solution, windshield washer fluids) and have a maintenance check on:** interior and exterior lights, oil, power steering fluid level, windshield wiper blade operation, safety warning lamps, brakes, ABS, air bags, safety belts, cooling system, battery connection, transmission fluid level, air filter. Have your windows completely clean on moving day and have a full tank of gas.

3. **Have emergency supplies.** When moving, it is nice to be able to take your most important valuables in the car with you instead of putting them on a moving van. When moving in the winter you should have emergency supplies with you in your vehicle and this may minimize room for some of your valuables. However, if you were to become stranded on the roadside in winter weather you would benefit from having these items with you: extra clothes, hats, gloves, a shovel, salt, spare tire, blanket, tire chains (if you have never put them on, practice before your move), road flares, first aid kit, snow brush scraper, toolbox, food, and water. Have these items easily accessible in your vehicle.

4. **Change your driving as the weather changes.** Keep your eye on the weather as moving day approaches and although you may be busy the morning of your move, check the weather for your travel route. Blizzards and snow are not the only problem, check for rain storms, ice, wind, slush, and fog. I'm from Pittsburgh, PA and although everyone living here knows that winter is coming, it seems every year when the first "black ice" happens there are tons of collisions. When it rains in the summer the road does not normally freeze and one can continue driving the speed limit, however, when the temperature is in the low 30's, slow down – there could be ice! Leave space between you and the vehicle ahead of you. Bright, sunny, snowy days can cause poor visibility, wearing sun glasses can help. Accelerate and stop gradually, easy on the brakes, and just go slower. Use extra caution when driving over bridges and passes because they freeze before roads do. Remember when driving in bad weather, safety is more important than being on time.

5. **Extra supplies and things you may have to do on moving day.** You may have snow on the ground on moving day or the ground might be wet from rain. If so, you will need to have a shovel on hand so – do not pack it. When moving in the winter, your door will most likely be propped open so the movers can carry furniture in and out. You will want to have warm clothes on, possibly gloves and a hat. It is a good idea to have your heat shut off the day after you move if you are moving in the winter so that you can stay warm on moving day. If you are moving to a cold area you will want to make sure that the heat will be turned on there as well. Having someone (real estate agent or landlord) check it the day before to make sure it is working is a good idea. Waking up early to shovel any walkways will be helpful especially if you have rented a moving truck.Time is money.Have salt on hand to cover the walkways so no one slips while walking or carrying heavy furniture. If there is snow on the road where the moving truck will park you might want to clear that as well, otherwise pick up or delivery could be delayed. If you are taking items to a storage facility, consider that since no one usually resides at a storage facility. Thus, on a snowy day it may not be plowed. Keep your shovel on hand. For bad weather days, I recommend two men in and two men out on moving day which prevents wet, snowy, and or muddy shoes from tracking mud in the house. However, if you do not have enough movers, you should purchase <u>carpet</u> <u>film</u> <u>protector</u> or carpet cover for moving. The difference between regular plastic or sheets and carpet covering is that it is specific for moving and has a slightly adhesive back so the material will not slide which will help protect against accidents. Lastly, if it is raining or snowing heavily you may want to cover your furniture especially mattresses and upholstered furniture. You can purchase shrink wrap or use any type of water repellent material.

6. **Hot chocolate, coffee and pizzas are a good idea on a winter move day too!** Planning ahead is crucial to make sure you have the pizza delivery number, coffee pot, and hot chocolate available! Due to the possibilities of the weather being very cold on moving day, arrange for small children to be somewhere else (relative or babysitter).

Getting Started

Post Office

Just like the utility companies, you will have to put an order in with your current post office to have your mail forwarded to your new address. They will forward your mail for one year. After one year, they will forward only first class mail to your new address. You can pick up a change-of-address form at your post office and just put your old address, new address, and the date when you would like your mail to stop being delivered to your old address. It is that easy! You can also change your address on the website **www.USPS.com.** This can be done six months before your move or a couple of weeks before you move. It does take the post office a week or so to process this form. If you turn it in less than a week before you move, you will take a chance of some of your mail being delivered to your old residence when you are no longer there. When you go to your post office and ask for a change-of-address form, make sure that they do not give you a stop-mail form. The change-of-address form is different and most often is inside a packet. It is also nice to get the change-of-address form from your post office well in advance because the packet usually contains coupons for moving companies, storage companies, truck rental companies, address labels, home decorating, cell phone plans, car insurance, etc. You can also forward catalogs that you receive with a form inside the change-of-address packet.

It is important to remember that it occasionally takes a while for mail to be forwarded to your new address. If you owe money to a creditor, you should make sure that they receive your monthly payment even if the bill does not arrive at your new address. This is why it is helpful to put copies of your credit card statements and addresses for individuals or companies to whom you owe money in your Move Folder. Make sure this folder stays with you when you move. My husband and I once had all of our household belongings stuck on a truck for 17 days; it was a good thing that we had all of our important and financial papers with us.

If you have important documents/items, like paycheck or investment information, that you will need immediately upon arriving at your new town and you are worried about not having an apartment, house, or post-office box, you may want to see if you can have them sent to your employer at your new location.

Insurance

Contact your insurance agent and let them know that you will be moving and eventually canceling your policy for your car insurance and homeowners/renters insurance. Keep paying your premium for your car insurance, if you do it monthly, until you sign a contract for your new car insurance. Your old car insurance will still cover you for 20 to 30 days. However, it is very important for you to open a new policy upon arrival in your new town. You cannot get car insurance in a new town unless you have an address. Once you have an address, the transition process should be easy, especially if your insurance company is national.

Contact your insurance company to make sure your household goods are covered during the move through your homeowners or renters policy. If not, find out how much the movers cover. Movers' basic insurance may cover items by pound, which may not be enough. See what additional insurance they offer. If your current homeowner's insurance covers your household and personal goods during the move, inquire if it will also cover your goods while they are in storage in case of a delay in moving in. It is not a good idea to close on selling your home and not have an apartment or house because you will have a gap during which you do not have any coverage on your household goods. You want to always have a policy in place to protect your household goods, even if they are in storage. If you are selling your house, do not cancel your homeowners insurance until after closing on another house or, if you are renting, until your rental insurance begins. Shop around for the best price on homeowners or renters insurance and make sure that your price will not change over time.

Speak to your insurance agent about your extraordinary items. Have them appraised and take pictures of these items (antiques, jewelry, paintings, etc.) in the event that you need to file an insurance claim. Mark down serial numbers of large electronic equipment and put the information in the move folder. The more valuable your items are, the more you will pay for insurance. Remember, as mentioned in the "Investigate" section, there may be language in your homeowners' policy that prohibits you from leaving a home vacant.

Healthcare Transfer

If you are relocating with your current employer, then most likely your healthcare will basically remain the same. You should speak to your human resource manager to find out what kinds of changes there may be, if any.

You should not go without healthcare coverage for any period of time. If you are resigning from your current job and you will be seeking employment in your new area, "Cobra" health insurance coverage should be available to you. This comprehensive healthcare coverage allows you to temporarily insure yourself and your family while you are seeking employment.

Getting Organized and Ready to Pack

It generally takes two weeks or more to pack your household goods. If you are employed full time and packing in the evenings, it may take even longer. Having designated areas for packed boxes, items for storage, items that you are personally taking with you, and items to be given or thrown away is a key in staying organized while moving. Designate a "packed-boxes room" (or area). It would usually be a room that is not used much and ideally on the ground floor. Remember, you may save money if you can have everything on the ground floor on moving day. If you are lucky enough to have a spare room with not much in it, empty it completely or move all of the items to one side. If you do not have a spare room, a dining room or any room that is not used much is a good place for packed boxes. You can push the table to one end and even stack boxes under and on top of the table. Fragile boxes can go on top. Now you are ready to start collecting "packing materials" and empty boxes. You can store these items temporarily in this room. Once you have certain items packed and are absolutely sure you will not need them, you can stack the packed boxes in this room. You will be taking empty boxes and packing materials out of the "packed-boxes room" and bringing back packed boxes to stack in this room. I do not recommend taping any boxes shut unless you are extremely sure that you will not need the items inside. I did not tape most boxes shut until the last week before moving just in case I needed something I had packed. I did tape shut boxes with holiday decorations, old books, and other items that I absolutely knew I would not need.

When you are ready to start packing, take a couple of empty boxes from the packed-boxes room and try to clear a space in each room of your house where you can keep the empty boxes. You can pack rooms slowly and leave boxes open in case you need something inside. It is smart to pack items from a particular room in the same box, for example, all bedroom items in three or four boxes with nothing else in the box from any other rooms. Mixing up items from different rooms can cause frustration when you are at your new residence and looking for items. I refer to this as "scatter packing."

If you have boxes that are going to a storage facility, they should be marked "storage" on several sides of the boxes. Keep these boxes separate from other boxes because they will most likely be dropped off first at the storage facility. Keeping them separate will help on moving day because you will want them to be loaded last so they can be dropped off first at the storage facility.

You should have a designated area for boxes and items that are going with you. I always liked to use a corner of my bedroom for this since these items are usually personal and expensive items. The few things that you have left in a room that you are still using, that is not packed (e.g., lamps, telephones, hangers) should have a designated box for them to be packed on moving day.

You should take care of items that you are going to give away or throw away as soon as you can. Getting them out of the way will give you more room to stay organized.

On moving day, you will need to make the movers aware that you have certain areas for boxes that are going to storage and let them know where the items that are going with you are so that they do not take them. All boxes should be marked with bold black ink. You will be writing storage, fragile, and this end up on the boxes as well as numbering them.

Your overall goal should be to get as many empty (packed) rooms, closets, or areas as you can. The closer and closer you get to moving day, you should have more and more of your rooms in your house empty (packed).

Throwing Away and Sorting Items

Eliminate items that you absolutely never use before moving, especially big, bulky and/or heavy items. There are a few items that I regret throwing away, so be cautious. If you are packing in a rush, you may make bad decisions about what to throw away. If you paid a lot of money for the item, you may want to keep it. Old appliances are good to tag along. You never know when your primary appliance will break or get damaged on a move, so it is good to have a back up.

Having a garage sale is a good idea, but it does involve time. A garage sale may compromise your time to get organized for your move. If you do not have much time to pack for the move, I recommend dropping off the items at a local donation center and getting a receipt for your taxes. You can also donate items to schools or libraries. Besides, bad weather could produce a poor turn out for your garage sale, and then you are stuck with all the items and no profit.

♲ Eco-Friendly Moving Tip

Clothes can be sorted and not necessarily thrown away. Clothes are great substitutes for that very expensive bubble wrap. Old T-shirts, sweat pants, coats or socks always worked fine for us as bubble wrap. We never broke one item! If you are moving in the summer, you can use those "winter clothes" (sealed in plastic) as bubble wrap. If you are moving in the winter, you can use summer clothes as bubble wrap, but they are not usually as thick and are not as good as winter clothes for cushioning. We will discuss this in detail in the "Smart Packing" section. Try to sort your clothes accordingly: good clothes should be packed. Clothes you can use for cushioning should go in the packed-boxes room, and clothes that you want to give away or sell should go in a bag or box labeled "Goodwill" or "Sell."

Buckets, bowls, and waste cans are great support inside boxes for crystal knickknacks, fragile dishes, lamp shades, or other fragile items. Do not throw away any item that may serve this purpose when you are sorting and throwing away items before you start packing. You can always toss the item after you move.

If you have 20 bath towels and use only 10, do not give or throw away the other 10. Old bath towels always worked well for us when packing pictures and mirrors. Your linen closet is full of bubble wrap! Sheets, blankets, tablecloths, old shower curtains, pillow cases, baby blankets, etc., can all be used as bubble wrap and/or extra cushioning. Put these items in your designated packed-boxes room so you can get them when you are ready to start packing. Try not to bury them under empty boxes. Once, I put a lot of towels and blankets in the "packed-boxes room" and then forgot about them until I was almost done packing! Make sure you don't make the same mistake! Ask friends, relatives and co-workers for their old sheets, comforters, blankets, and towels. This is an inexpensive way to collect cushioning for packing fragile items.

Be a Frugal Mover!

I have spoken to a lot of people who have moved, and they threw away a lot, saying that they would repurchase at their new place. You never know what your finances will be like once you move. Remember, you have to buy new cleaning products, food, bath products, home decorations, paint, etc. You just do not know what kind of costs you will have after you move. Being frugal when you are moving is wise.

Hazardous Materials

Schedule some time to look for "hazardous materials." Your moving company, whether you are renting a truck or hiring a moving company, should provide you with a list of hazardous materials that cannot go on a truck. Airlines have restrictions on transporting hazardous material as well. Unfortunately, you will have to throw away or give away hazardous materials that cannot be taken in a car or truck or on an airplane for safety reasons. These restrictions should be taken very seriously. Some materials have special waste procedures and may have to be taken to a hazardous waste site, so you may want to eliminate them well in advance before moving day. Most Yellow Pages have lists for waste recycling and disposal or look online. Some hazardous materials include but are not limited to the following.

Hazardous Materials List

aerosol cans	compressed gases	motor oil
alcohol/wine	corrosives	nail polish and remover
ammunition	explosives	oil
automotive repair	fire extinguishers	oxidizers
batteries	fireworks	oxygen bottles
bleach	firearms	paint thinners
bottled gas	flammable liquids/solids	varnish
candles	gasoline	poisons
cleaning fluids	kerosene and lighter fluid	propane cylinders
chemicals	maintenance chemicals	radioactive materials
detergents	matches and lighters	radio-pharmaceuticals

Besides hazardous materials, there are other items that moving companies are not permitted to take on their truck, such as:

animals	live plants (ask driver)
candles (if going to storage)	medications
garbage	perishable foods
jewelry	stamp and coin collections
legal documents	oil paintings

Things to Buy and Collect

 Eco-Friendly Moving Tip

Newspaper and gloves

If you are on a tight moving budget, wrapping your dishes in newspaper can save you money. Newspaper is a great source of protection to wrap dishes and glass items. Newspaper sheds a lot of ink, so I would recommend it only for wrapping dishes or items that you can clean. I always washed any dishes before using them if I had wrapped them in newspaper during a move. If you are concerned about your dishes getting ink on them, you can purchase a roll or two of white generic paper towels and wrap the dish in the paper towel before covering it with newspaper. I usually collected about a foot-high pile of newspaper for one set of dishes (eight-piece setting) and various other glass bowls and odd pieces. You should wear latex gloves when working with newspaper or your hands will get ink on them. If wrapped correctly and placed in the box correctly with adequate packing around them, your dishes should not break when wrapped in newspaper. I never broke any dishes when moving, and if you follow my directions in the "Smart Packing" section of this book, you won't either.

If you have money to spend on packing supplies and/or you are concerned about getting ink on your dishes, you can buy "unbleached packing paper" from a moving supply company or a wholesale moving supply company. For your most fragile items, you can purchase bubble wrap as well.

Boxes

There are many moving-box calculators on line that will determine how many boxes you will need for your move. All you have to do is insert the number of bedrooms that you have, and the calculation will be done for you. Another good way to estimate how many boxes you will need is to count the rooms and closets in your house. A room or closet may take four or five boxes, depending on how full it is. If you have 10 rooms and closets, you will need roughly 50 boxes (10 X 5 = 50). Plus, you should have six to ten "last-minute boxes" on hand for the day of the move. Last minute-boxes are for items that you will be using up until the morning that you are moving. For example, your toaster, telephones, drapes, lamps, night lights, cooking utensils, coffee pot, a few plates and cups, towels, hair dryer, toilet paper, facial tissue, shower curtains, soap, etc. Your last-minute boxes will become your "open-first boxes" at your new place, giving you the essentials you will need right away. It can be hard to judge how much you will be able to transport in the car or truck that you are driving on moving day. If you have over judged the amount that you can transport, you will need empty last-minute boxes to put items in quickly for the movers to load on the truck. Make sure that you have empty boxes available on moving day!

Eco-Friendly Moving Tip

Obtaining Boxes

Buying moving boxes is recommended for two reasons. First, moving boxes are very thick and strong. Second, moving boxes usually come in three sizes: small, medium, and large. Having just three different size boxes will make it easier to pack your moving truck tight to avoid shifting and damage. If you have many different size boxes, you may have more "gaps" on your moving truck, which will increase your chance of damage to your household goods.

However, if your budget does not permit you to buy moving boxes, you can call your local grocery store in the evening and ask for the stockroom manager to see if they will give you some empty boxes. Most stockroom employees are glad to give them away because they do not have to cut them up for the trash. Avoid produce boxes because they may not be clean. Ask if they can save some egg and paper towel boxes for you. Egg boxes should not be used if you see broken egg residue. Egg boxes are thicker boxes that are ideal for dishes. Paper towel boxes are the largest boxes that a grocery store usually has. You can also get very sturdy small boxes at a liquor store. These boxes will most likely still have cellular dividers inside them (used to divide the liquor bottles), which are great for packing delicate champagne and wine glasses, (see the "Smart Packing" section). You can buy cellular dividers from most moving supply companies as well. I obtained boxes from grocery stores many times and never received an unclean one; they are usually in very good condition.

When I first moved, I was very move-naïve. I thought that a box was either in its correct form or it was cut up and was junk. I learned from my husband that you can break boxes down correctly so they can be stored without taking up a lot of space and used again and again! When you go to a packing store and buy moving boxes, you get them flat, and you can flatten any box and open it back up again to reuse. So, when you are picking boxes up from the grocery store, you can break them down to get a lot of them in your vehicle, and you can store them in their broken-down state in your packed-boxes area/room. When you are opening the boxes and getting ready to pack them, I suggest taping the bottoms on the inside and on the outside. Three strips of mailing/packaging tape along the split will give you the best support.

Some people like to "tuck" boxes shut. I recommend taping them shut just like the boxes are taped when you receive a package in the mail from a company. If you tuck them, they could come loose. Also, a box that is merely tucked shut is an invitation for theft as well. If you both tuck and tape them, the tuck leaves air and your tape does not lie flat to the cardboard. So, fold the box shut neatly—short ends in, then long ends in—and then tape the box on the crease.

Properly Taped Shut

Incorrectly "Tucked" Shut

If you have purchased moving boxes at a moving supply company or from the mover you have hired and you do not use all of them, you can usually return the unused ones. When moving, especially if you are packing yourself and having a moving truck pick up your shipment, it is best to have big boxes. We made the mistake once of putting very small boxes (10 inches by 15 inches) and a small bundled item on a moving van, and we lost them both. The commercial moving vans usually have several other customers' boxes on their van with your boxes. If a truck stops fast or turns quickly, your small boxes may shift away from the rest of your items. So, avoid small boxes and/or small items if a moving company is moving you. Do not pack boxes too heavy. A range of 30 to 40 pounds per box is recommended. Some boxes are more sturdy and can hold more weight. Use your judgment and do not overpack boxes, or you may encounter breakage.

Mailing Boxes

If your spouse, friends, or relatives are already at your new destination, consider mailing items in boxes to your new home. If you are planning on mailing anything to your new residence, remember that there are restrictions for mailing boxes. If you are taking the box to the post office, it cannot be over 50 pounds. You are not permitted to mail anything in a liquor box if the liquor label/advertising is showing on the box. You can cover the box with a plain paper bag to avoid seeing the advertising. It is not recommended to mail liquid in a box in case the container would rupture or a lid would come loose. Once a box is delivered, it may sit outside for some time before someone is able to collect it. Damage can occur if you are mailing photos or plastic items to a climate that is very hot or very cold. If you are mailing books, ask for the "media mail rate." The entire contents of the box must be books to get this rate. Books are heavy so make sure the box is taped shut very well. Make sure that the address that you are mailing the box to and your return address are on the box and they are legible.

Things to Buy List

General List for a 3-4 room home around 2,600 square feet.

1. **Brown folder and notebook** - for all important move-related papers/receipts.

2. **Clear mailing/packaging tape** - Buy six to eight rolls of clear mailing/packaging tape. Buy extra because not only will you be taping boxes shut, you will be taping cardboard and cushioning around glass, furniture legs, televisions, etc., if you are doing your own crating.

3. **10 small moving boxes** - You can buy them or get boxes from liquor stores.

4. **20 medium moving boxes** - Buy them or get them from a grocery store.

5. **10 very large moving boxes** -You can buy them or you can use paper towel boxes from grocery stores.

6. **Permanent black markers** - to label boxes.

7. **Pack of ink pens** - for Box Number Sheets.

8. **Latex gloves** - to protect your hands if you are using newspaper to pack dishes.

9. **Several rolls of paper towels** - for cleaning on move day. Before covering dishes with newspaper, you can use paper towels to protect dishes from ink. Tissue paper works to protect dishes also.

10. **Paper plates and plastic forks** - for meals on moving day!

11. **Bottled water**

12. **Large garbage bags** - 1 box for trash

13. **Newspaper** - (foot-high stack) or unprinted packaging paper (can get from a wholesale moving supply company).

14. **Rope** - If you are renting a truck that has tie down rings on the interior walls, you can secure furniture to the walls with rope.

15. **Box cutters** - to make unpacking easier.

16. **Sealable plastic baggies** - to store small parts (nuts, bolts, screws) from electronics and appliances. Tape bags to the back of the appliance. Also for transporting food.

17. **Ratchet Straps with hooks (6)** - for securing a load in a rental truck. You can purchase these at an automotive store.

18. **Stretch wrap** - to cover furniture.

19. **Furniture pads -** Two or three for each piece of furniture. Rental truck company furniture pads are usually thinner than the professional moving company pads.

20. **Carpet protection plastic -** to protect carpet if there is bad weather (adheres to carpet to avoid slipping; not recommended for hardwood flooring).

You may not need to purchase everything on this list. If you are hiring a full-service moving company to pack, load, and transport your belongings, you will need very few items on this list. However, if you are renting a truck and moving yourself, you will need everything on this list. For a customized move, you will have to determine what you need to accommodate your specific situation. Also, speak to your moving company to see what they supply and if there is an extra cost for supplies.

Smart Packing

Box Number Sheets

A rough estimate for a two-bedroom household would be 35 to 40 boxes. Online moving box calculators or packing calculators are available to determine how many boxes you need. However, the accuracy can fluctuate depending on your lifestyle habits, such as your tendency to collect and your personal gauge for what is "a lot."

Once you have boxes and are ready to start packing, you may want to use a numbering system, a method to keep track of what is inside each box. We came up with this idea on our second move. We taped a Box Number Sheet to every box that we used for packing. The sheet had a number on the top of it, and we wrote that number on the box that we taped it to. Underneath the box number on the sheet, there was a list of blank lines. The open box sat in a room, and as we put items inside the box, we listed them on the Box Number Sheet, which was taped to the side of the box.

Once the box was full, we would transfer the box to the packed boxes room with the Box Number Sheet still attached to it. If the box contained only items from a specific room, we would also write on the box "Bedroom" or "Bathroom" with bold black marker in addition to the number on the box. The movers appreciate room names on boxes, as this helps them in placing boxes in the appropriate rooms. If they are delivering to your upstairs, they will put the boxes in their specific rooms.

If a box was not completely full, I would leave the box untaped with the Box Number Sheet still attached so that I could add more items. A few days before moving, you will want to collect all the Box Number Sheets from the boxes and then tape the boxes shut. We kept all of the Box Number Sheets in our move folder. These sheets are your personal detailed inventory listing of what is contained in each box. I do not recommend taping boxes shut too soon because it is likely that you will need something that has been packed. I wasted a lot of tape ripping boxes open to find items. By leaving the Box Number Sheets attached to the boxes, you will know just exactly what is in all of the packed boxes in case you need an item. It is also nice to leave them open in case you want to put another item in the box.

Once you get to your new place and the movers bring your household goods, you may feel overwhelmed. Unpacking is just as time consuming as packing. I remember just wanting a cup of coffee. We just looked through our Box Number Sheets and found "coffee pot"! We knew exactly what number box it was in, so all we had to do was find that box. It is also a good idea to write the box number in bold, black marker on at least two sides of the box so you can locate it quickly. The Box Number Sheet method works very well.

(A Box Number Sheet is provided at the end of this book for you to make copies for your boxes.) It is wonderful to know where everything is!

If you are packing in a hurry, you may start putting items in boxes and forget to list them on the Box Number Sheet that is taped to the outside of the box. However, if you are not "scatter packing" and you are keeping room items together, you will have an idea what box the item you are looking for may be in. For example, if you need a tie or a bathrobe upon arriving at your new residence and you did not list it on the Box Number Sheet, you can look for boxes marked "bedroom." However, if you have five or six bedroom boxes, then you have some work ahead of you but much less than if you did not mark the boxes at all. I highly recommend trying to list most items that you pack in a box on the Box Number Sheet on the outside of the box to avoid chaos and stress. You can buy a pack of pens and keep one in every room so when you are packing, you have a pen available to list items on the Box Number Sheets. If you have a box that is only half full, definitely leave it untaped because you may have a last minute item that can fit in the box. For example, if a bathroom box is half full, remember that you may have a shower curtain, toilet paper, or cleaning products that you can put in there. Boxes that are getting too heavy but are not full can remain open for a "light item" such as a box of envelopes, a plastic container, a plastic tray, etc.

You may find that months after you move, you will still have boxes that are taped shut. These tend to be boxes with books, out of season clothes or holiday decorations. Do not put an important item in with boxes that you may not open right away. You most likely will forget what box you put it in.

General Packing Rules

1. Do not pack any items that you think you may need while you are in between homes and/or for traveling to your new home (see Survival List).

2. Always count on the longest "drop-off window" so you are prepared with enough items to make your time in between homes comfortable.

3. If you have chosen to use unprinted packing paper as cushioning on the bottoms of your boxes, be generous because it absorbs shock.

4. Put heavier items in smaller boxes and lighter items in larger boxes, and if you are putting heavy items in with lighter items then put the heavier items on the bottom and the lighter items on top. If the box gets turned upside down, the lighter items on top may get smashed. Make sure the lighter item(s) are not fragile.

5. Do not overfill a box. The top should close easily without bulging.

6. Any items that you are packing that might be in storage for a while or might not be opened for awhile should be put into a plastic bag before being put into the box to protect the items from picking up a "cardboard box" smell and to protect the items from water damage if an unforeseen event should occur.

7. Avoid very small boxes and loose items that are unboxed for moves over 500 miles. Your household goods may be loaded onto a moving truck, taken to a warehouse where they will be unloaded, then loaded again when there is a truck available to transport your items to their final destination. During loading and unloading, it is easy for small boxes and unboxed items to get lost.

What to Pack First

Books/Magazines/Videos

Packing heavier items first is a good idea because you can stack lighter boxes on top. Some items I packed and taped shut early are books, magazines, videos, and knickknacks. I used grocery-store egg boxes because they are strong and can support the heavy books. For books, you can also use liquor boxes from your local liquor store, which are also very strong. Egg boxes are usually a little bigger than the liquor boxes. Lay books flat in the box so the spines won't break. You can put 10 to 20 books in a box and then lift to see if it is getting too heavy. Anyone who is not used to lifting heavy objects or anyone with a back problem should be very careful not to pack boxes too heavy. Even though movers may be taking your boxes, you will still be lifting it to move it to where your packed boxes are, and you will be lifting the boxes at your new residence. You do not have to pack a book box completely full you can fill the empty half with light items (papers, office supplies, envelopes) to avoid making it too heavy and causing it to rupture. This way, you will not waste space by leaving the box half empty. Make sure that you do not put anything fragile in with books just in case the box is turned upside down during the move. Remember, if you have children and are traveling by car or plane to your new home, you may want to leave some kids books/coloring books out to take for the trip on move day.

Photos

You should pack photo albums and pictures early; however, you should transport these items yourself because you do not want to risk losing your precious memories. Put these packed items in a designated spot in your bedroom with other items that are going with you to your new residence and make sure that the movers or helpers do not accidentally take them.

Household Decorations

If you are not planning on entertaining before you move, knick knacks, pictures, or any house decorations should be packed first. Knickknacks can be wrapped in newspaper and put inside another household item. For example, any vase or decorative pitcher can be filled with newspaper, and a smaller wrapped knickknack can be put inside.

Holiday Decorations

Most often holiday items are already packed in your attic or closet; however, if there is ceramic or glass inside, you will want to repack the box with proper cushioning around fragile items to avoid breaks. Also, it is important to use a new box if the box the items are in is older and not sturdy. Remember that movers do not know what is inside your boxes, so unless you mark the box "Fragile," they may toss it to the rear of the truck or put it in an area of the truck where it may shift during travel.

Other items that you can pack first:

- China
- Old computers
- Secondary televisions
- Stereos and speakers
- Tapes, CDs, and DVDs
- Old camcorders
- Musical equipment
- Folding tables and chairs
- Sports equipment

Seasonal Packing

Your list of items to pack first will be different depending on whether you are moving in the summer or the winter.

If you are moving in the winter, pack these items first:

- Summer sports equipment
- Outdoor furniture (pack cushions in box)
- Outdoor grill
- Summer clothes (see Using Clothing Packed In Plastic Bags For Cushioning)
- Summer shoes
- Gardening equipment
- Outdoor toys
- Pool items

If you are moving in the summer, pack these items first:

- Winter sports equipment

- Winter toys

- Winter clothes

- Winter shoes

- Holiday decorations

Outdoor Grill

The propane tank on a grill must be removed. You can return the tank and ask for a credit slip to pick up a new one in your new town if there is a franchise store. If you are taking your propane tank, you should have it professionally sealed.

Pool Trunk

If you have a swimming pool, you may have an area where you keep your pool supplies or an outdoor pool trunk that holds all of your pool supplies (rafts, balls, water toys, floats, etc.). These items can be packed early if it is not swimming season. If you are taking the pool trunk, then you may just have to add a few items to it, such as your pool cover. If you are not taking the pool trunk, then you will have to remove all items and put them into boxes. You will be unable to transport any pool chemicals.

 Eco-Friendly Moving Tip

Packing Your Clothes

Clothing can pick up a cardboard-box smell from being in boxes, especially in high heat. One time the moving company that we hired did not go into detail about their delivery window. (I highly recommend getting the delivery window in writing before you sign a moving contract.) Our shipment was not delivered to us for 17 days, and I had packed clothing in cardboard boxes. It was in the middle of the summer, and my clothes picked up a smell from the cardboard boxes that was very hard to get out. After that move, I refused to ever put clothing in cardboard boxes again unless they were in a plastic bag with all the air pressed out and a twist tie securing the bag. I never got that smell in my clothes again. You can use a vacuum-cleaner hose to suck the air out of the plastic bag! Be careful not to suck up any clothing.

Clothes can be separated into groups. If you are working, you will need to keep out the clothes that you wear to work. However, we all have those good clothes that we like but never wear. These clothes along with out-of-season clothes should be packed early in plastic bags and then put into boxes. Old clothes and clothes that you may give away or throw away can actually be used as packing material around small fragile items. One of my favorite little tricks is to put little knick knacks inside thick socks and then put them inside shoes. I then put belts and purses in with the shoes as well. I never broke one knickknack, and this idea is a real space saver! Also, you can use old T-shirts around wine glasses that are in dividers inside of liquor boxes.

Using Clothing Packed in Plastic Bags for Cushioning
Moving companies will sometimes suggest when packing fragile items to use four inches of unprinted packaging paper for cushioning on the bottom of boxes, each item to be individually wrapped in unprinted packaging paper, crushed unprinted packaging paper around each item and crushed unprinted packaging paper on top of the items. Are you moving your household goods or a box of unprinted packaging paper? You can save a lot of money by using your clothes, towels, blankets, and pillows for cushioning. You will use fewer boxes as well.

Clothes packed in plastic bags can serve as cushioning for other items when packing. They can be used as great cushioning for fragile items or on the bottom or top of dishes in a box. Winter clothes—such as coats, sweaters, sweatshirts, scarves, hats—sealed in plastic make very good cushioning in boxes. You can wrap an 8x10 picture frame with glass in a box with a plastic bag of clothing on the bottom. Stand the picture up vertically and put more cushioning, like a pillow or blanket, around it. You will also need cushioning, such as a winter coat, on top of the picture. Do not forget to mark the box "Fragile." I also recommend that any pillows or blankets used as cushioning be sealed in plastic to avoid picking up a smell from the box.

Before you start packing, you should take a rough inventory of how many fragile items you have. How many large winter coats, comforters, pillows, and blankets do you have that can be used to cushion these fragile items? You may need to purchase some bubble wrap if you do not have a lot of clothes that you can use as cushioning.

Dishes

Dishes are one of the most tedious items to pack. I did buy bubble wrap for some of my most precious dishes. However, bubble wrap is expensive and gets used up fast. The majority of my dishes were wrapped in a white napkin or tissue to protect them from ink, then wrapped with newspaper, and finally taped on the ends. Taping is optional.

Your goal is to get as much cushioning around the dishes as possible, and once they are stacked in the box, the newspaper will firmly stay in place. I was always very successful with moving my dishes. Since dishes are heavy, I liked to use the heavier egg boxes (from a grocery store) or wine boxes (from a liquor store). You can take a thick blanket and fold it to the size of the bottom of the box, put it in a garbage bag, squeeze out the air, and twist tie it shut. Put this bagged blanket on the bottom of the box. If you are using newspaper, I suggest wearing latex gloves to protect your hands from the ink on the newspaper. I would also cover the table that you will be working on.

For a dinner plate, you should use two full-size pieces of newspaper. Open them up and lay them directly on top of each other. Take your plate and cover it with two napkins or tissue paper to protect it from the ink (optional). Once the plate is covered, place it in the middle of the newspaper as if you were going to serve food on it and fold all ends in toward the middle of the plate (where you would put food), folding the ends until they come together in the middle.

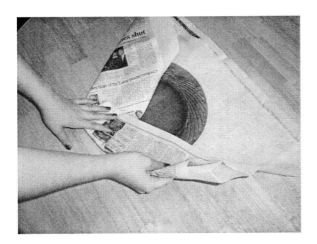 

Folding the newspaper and tissue paper around the plate then taping it.

Now you can tape where you are holding the ends together. Tape the plate from one end of the plate through the middle to wrap around the opposite end. However, using tape is optional because stacking the wrapped dishes will hold the newspaper in place.

You will see that you have a lot of cushioning on the one side of the plate and none on the back side. This is alright because you are going to stack them vertically and the front cushion on one plate will act as cushioning on the back of another plate! If you are concerned about the lack of cushioning on the back side of the plate you can flip it and wrap it again. This will give you cushioning on both sides. I did this for very good china. **Never lay plates flat in a box without cushioning or they will break.**

Securing the Dishes in the Box

After you wrap half a dozen plates, you can start stacking them up in the box that has the bagged blanket on the bottom. Here is where your old clothes or towels come in handy. Use these items around the sides of the plates and in the fronts and backs of the last plates in the row to hold them secure and provide the needed cushioning. Dish towels and pot holders come in handy here too, and you will be keeping kitchen items together! Just remember to leave a couple out for your last-minute cooking. You should not have any voids or cavities in a box with dishes. Remember, you will need height on top of the plates for cushioning, so if your plates stack to the top of the box, you may need a deeper box. Other boxes may get stacked on top of these boxes; therefore, you need cushioning inside on top of the dishes for protection. Once all of the plates are secured and cushioned in the box, prepare a cushion for the top. It may be a throw pillow from the living room (this is a case where "scatter packing" is a good thing), or maybe a winter coat. Pillows are great on top of your fragile items. Remember to seal these cushions in plastic to protect them from getting a "box" smell if they are going to be in the box for any duration. Follow this same concept for smaller plates and bowls, and stack them on edge vertically as well. Mark these boxes "Fragile" on all sides.

Glasses and Cups

Wrap a napkin around the glass to protect it from the newspaper ink and tape. For taller drinking glasses, use one sheet of newspaper folded in half. Lay the newspaper flat on a table and then lay the glass down on its side on one end. There should be several inches of newspaper extending from each end of the glass. Fold the one end of the newspaper where the glass is and start rolling the newspaper tightly around the glass. Secure the newspaper tightly with tape on the side of the glass so it does not come loose. Now you can tuck in the ends, and you won't need to use tape.

Rolling a glass in tissue and newspaper then tucking in the ends.

Glasses must also be placed in a box vertically with the rim down and with plenty of cushioning around them to hold them upright. You can stack a few glasses after they are wrapped. Wine boxes with the cellular dividers still in them are great for tall glasses, wine glasses, and flutes. You can even use a six-pack case from beer to secure wrapped glasses in a box. Place the wrapped glasses in the sections and put cushioning around them with pieces of crumbled newspaper, old socks, tank tops or small T-shirts. Coffee cups can be rolled the same way as glasses. You can also use your out-of-season scarves, hats, and gloves as cushioning for dishes if it is a summer move.

Once the box is filled with glasses and cushion is placed around the sides, check your kitchen for tiny fragile items to put inside the glasses. For example, a shot glass can be wrapped in newspaper and put inside a wrapped glass. You can put utensils in the glasses and around them, be creative! Emptying those drawers is your goal! Remember, if you are using a box with cellular dividers, you still need cushioning on the bottom and top of the item you are putting in the divided section. Make sure that the item is wrapped with plenty of cushioning on the ends or use a sock at the bottom of each divided section.

Putting wrapped crystal flutes into dividers in a box.

Crystal and China

These items should be packed in a smaller box, bucket, bowl, or trash can and then placed in a larger box. You will want to wrap the item preferably in bubble wrap or some type of cushioning and secure with tape. Then place the item in a small container and surround it with cushioning. Then place it in a larger box. This is the best way to secure china and crystal.

Pots and Pans

When packing pots and pans, remember use can use these items as security for well-wrapped crystal items/dishes. Wrap the crystal item in a paper towel, roll it in newspaper or bubble wrap, and then tape the ends. Take a pot holder and wrap it around the item and place it in the pot. You will want to put something on top of the pot such as a cutting board or a plastic container. Remember to use your pots and plastic containers for your fragile kitchen items! In the kitchen, you can pack items early that you do not use often, e.g., steamer or an old coffee pot, and it helps to do so. Remember not to pack boxes too heavy. Do not use any plastic containers that you may need to transport food from your refrigerator.

Small Appliances

Wrap small appliances such as blenders and coffee makers in a bath towel, packaging paper, or bubble wrap. Place item in a small box, bucket, or waste can with a layer of cushioning on the bottom, sides, and top. Pot holders and dish towels are good side and top support for small appliances. This small box can then be placed into a larger box with other items. Mark the outer box "This End Up" to keep the appliance positioned properly.

Large Appliances

Stoves. Unplug or remove stoves from gas supply. Loose parts should be wrapped and put inside. Check the owner's manual or call the appliance center for special instructions before you begin to pack a large appliance. You can tape any parts that may come loose, like electrical cords, to the back of the appliance. Make sure that during the move, the appliance is positioned properly.

Refrigerators and Freezers. Slow down on buying food a few weeks before you move, and use up what you have in your pantry and refrigerator. Clean your refrigerator two to three days before you move. If you have plastic containers with food in them, remember that they have to be washed and packed if you plan on keeping them. Once your refrigerator is clean; plan a meal or buy lunch meat for sandwiches on moving day, and buy only what you will need for the next few days. Refrigerators can be unplugged just before you move them; however, you may have to wait 24 hours to use them after transporting and arriving at your new place. Call the manufacturer of your refrigerator or read the owner's manual for these specifics on your model. On moving day, you can put sandwiches in a cooler on ice or have a plan for where you will stop for a meal. If you are going to order food, make sure that you have the phone number and menu available for moving day. You may have packed or thrown away menus and won't have them available so be prepared. If you are taking any food with you, make sure that the lids are on tight; secure any opened packages by putting them in another sealable plastic bag. Any glass jars should be put into a sealable plastic bag and then wrapped in cushioning. If your freezer is packed with frozen food, you should start defrosting and eating those items a month or more before. It is very hard to transport frozen foods. If you have a second, separate freezer, you could work on emptying that one first. Once your freezer is empty, it must be defrosted and allowed to dry for 24 hours prior to loading.

Washers and Dryers. Washers and dryers must be disconnected and serviced. Hoses must be properly disconnected from the wall, drained, and sealed off with a plastic bag and rubber band. At most storage and/or packing supply companies, you can purchase special inserts to brace the tub and secure the spring-mounted motor of your washer during transport. When a washer is removed, there can be water underneath it. If you are in an apartment, you will most likely have to clean it up before you leave, so be prepared with paper towels and cleaning products. If you are not taking your washer and dryer, make sure that they are empty!

Beer Tubs and Coolers. These containers are great to transport cleaning products in. Make sure all caps are tightened. If the bottles leak, the liquids and powders will be contained inside the cooler. A bottle that leaks inside a box will most likely cause the box to rip apart. Keep all liquids together, and do not pack anything with the liquids that would get ruined. A plastic bathroom waste can lined with a plastic bag is great for transporting shampoos, soaps, etc. After you fill it, twist tie the bag shut, put another plastic bag around the outside, and twist tie that bag shut. You can then put it into a box. Remember not to transport hazardous materials. It is dangerous to have them in the car with you.

Laundry Baskets. Laundry baskets always kind of stumped me. You can just stack them together, and the movers will "tag them" and put them in the truck. Or you can put them inside a large paper-towel box that you get from a grocery store to function as cushioning for fragile items. For example, you can remove the legs of a small armoire and put a blanket around the top piece. Then put it inside the laundry basket inside the box. You can wrap the legs in a towel and put them on the sides of the top piece. I would then put other items in the box that were not too heavy such as T-shirts or out-of-season clothes (sealed in a plastic bag). Look around before you close a box that still has room in it. You may be able to fit some knickknacks or wrapped pictures, etc., inside.

It is easy to overlook the clothes in your laundry room. Remember that you have to pack them! You can put them in garbage bags and use them as cushioning on the bottom of boxes for fragile items.

Linen Box. I do not recommend using good sheets for cushioning because they are too thin. You should pack your good bedding and linens in a plastic garbage bag, squeeze out the air and tie it with a twist tie. By keeping them clean, you will save yourself from having to wash them at your new place. There is an awful lot to do when you arrive at a new place, and you do not want to have to rewash all of your good bedding and linens. Your linen box is important because you will want to put clean sheets on your beds the first night that you sleep in your new residence. Make sure that you know exactly what box the sheets are in. You may even want to take a few sheet sets with you personally so you do not have to search for them upon arrival.

Helpful Ideas for Children

If you have children who will be leaving friends and changing schools, there are a few things that you can do to help ease the sadness and anxiety. One is to ask the school if they could help with making a "Goodbye Video." Your child or the teacher can take video of all your child's classmates and teachers. They can videotape the front of the school, the classrooms, the art room, the gym, the lunch room, etc. When your child gets lonely for his old friends and school, he can watch the video. Secondly, you can have your child take an address book to school, and with the teacher's permission, it can be passed around for all the classmates to write down their street addresses, email addresses, and phone numbers. Your child will enjoy getting emails, text or even letters from his or her old friends and may even develop longtime friendships! See the "Post Move" section at the end of this book for "Don't Break The Chain," another helpful tip to ease the stress on children.

What to Pack Last

Kids' Rooms

If you have children, they are probably a little uncomfortable with the thoughts of moving. You can pack their out-of-season clothes, which you may already have in a room other than their room anyway. You can pack some of the toys that they do not use a lot and some of the clothes that they do not wear a lot. However, to save them added stress, try to pack their rooms last. If your children have suitcases, you can pack clothes for the move in them and some of their favorite toys, books, games, etc. It may take you just a few hours to get to your new location or it may take a day or two. If your child has a suitcase packed with clothes, pajamas, a few toys or things to do, their goodbye video and address book, they will not have to wait for you to locate these items once you arrive. Having a few of their loved and favorite things with them can comfort them.

Electronics

The television is an item that most people pack last. All televisions and electronics must be disconnected. It is a good idea to put any nuts, bolts, or screws into a plastic bag and tape them to the back of the television or appliance that you are disconnecting. Wrap any wires and bind with a twist tie or tape wires to the back of the item. They will be right there when it is time to reassemble it. You can always screw them back into the holes after disassembling if you do not want to bag them. Put any remotes in the box with televisions, DVRs, gaming devices, blu-ray and DVD players, etc.

It is ideal to be able to pack electronic equipment in original boxes with original packing. However, if you are unable to do this, you should wrap the item in bubble wrap or an old towel and then place the item in a slightly larger box with cushioning underneath and bubble wrap or another thick cushioning material all around the sides and top of the item. Do not forget cushioning on the top in case another heavy item is placed on top during the move. If your children have a lot of stuffed animals, you can put them into plastic bags and place them in front of the television screen in the box for protection. Pillows will work if you do not have stuffed animals. A television should be transported in an upright position and never laid down. If you do not have a box for your television or any other large appliances, ask the movers if they will pad them.

Keep in mind that if the movers have to disassemble (and/or reassemble) any electronics, you may pay extra. Also, any electronics that contain personal information such as tablets, laptops, iPods, etc. should be transported with you personally.

Specialty Items

Items such as pool tables, grandfather clocks, chandeliers, hot tubs, all need special packing. If you are nervous about breaking them, most moving companies can help you with these items for an additional fee. Read the owner's manuals for transporting instructions.

Kitchen Items

You will be using your kitchen until the night before the move. I always packed the majority of my dishes but left a couple of plates, glasses, coffee cups, and some silverware out. I packed pots, pans, and utensils that I hardly ever used several weeks ahead. I packed china and other kitchen odds and ends way ahead of time. I still had a working kitchen up until the day before moving and packed it very last in a "last-minute box." You can mark this box "kitchen and last minute" and you will know to open it first at your new place to get your new kitchen operating immediately.

Telephones

For safety reasons, pack your telephones last. Although it would be a rare event, you do not want to be alone in a room in your house, have an accident, and not be able to crawl to a phone because you packed it last week. Phones should go in a "last-minute box" on moving day. It is also a good idea to take a landline telephone in the car or in your Survival box so that you can plug in a phone to a phone jack in the wall immediately at your new residence before the movers arrive with your shipment.

Cable Box and Computer Modem—Beware!

You will have to call to schedule a date to have your cable shut off prior to moving. However, you may still want to watch TV up until the night before you move (to check the weather, keep kids occupied, etc.) Remember, you may have to return that cable box! We forgot to do this once, and when the movers arrived, we ended up taking it with us because we did not want to leave it there. Then we had to drive it back to our previous state and return it a few weeks later. Cable boxes are expensive, and the cable companies will bill you if you keep one. Call the company and find the nearest service center and hours of operation so you can drop it off on move day or the preferably the day before.

Computers

Computers must be disconnected. However, prior to disconnecting, you should back up your files. Remember to transport this important back-up disc with you personally when you move. Just like electronics, original packing is preferable when transporting computers. If you do not have the original packaging, computers should be wrapped in bubble wrap or an old towel and have plenty of cushioning around them. Place them into a box with cushioning on the bottom and then put cushioning on the top and sides. Do not use loose-fill or foam peanuts when packing computers. This material could generate static electricity that could damage your computer. If you have Internet service with either a cable, phone, or satellite company, you are responsible for returning the modem or associated devices before you move if you do not own them.

Crating Items—Large Paintings, Mirrors and Glass

You can have your moving company professionally crate items such as mirrors, paintings, or glass shelves. There will most likely be an extra fee for this. I went to help a friend pack her china and dishes once, and she was shocked to learn that her china cabinet doors had to come off and the shelves had to come out. Glass doors and shelves must be removed and "crated" to prevent breakage during a move. If you want to crate an item yourself, such as a mirror or piece of glass, you can take two pieces of thick cardboard and cut them slightly larger than the item. You can also use thin wood if you have the right size pieces. To support glass during transport, you can make an X across the glass with masking tape to help prevent a break. We also wrapped the corners in cardboard. Then wrap the mirror in large bubble wrap, a furniture blanket, or an old thick blanket, comforter, or sleeping bag. Lay the mirror on one piece of cardboard. Put another piece of cardboard on top, and then wrap packaging or mailing tape around the entire top, middle, and bottom of both pieces of cardboard. Use a lot of tape to make sure the mirror inside is very secure.

Make certain that the movers know that this is a very fragile item by marking "fragile—mirror" on both sides of the cardboard. Stand the mirror vertically against a wall away from where people walk until you are ready to move or the movers arrive on moving day. These items should be placed vertically in the moving truck between two mattresses. Tape is fine to use on cardboard or around old blankets that you do not intend on using again. Do not use tape, especially duct tape, around good blankets; it can leave a sticky, hard-to-remove residue. If you want to use tape to tightly support an item that is covered in a comforter, you can put an old sheet around the comforter to protect it from the tape's sticky residue. You can throw the sheet away at your new place and your comforter will be undamaged. I have even used strips of newspaper under tape to protect blankets from the sticky residue of tape. I prefer tape to rope to hold items secure. We never broke any of our mirrors through all of our moves. Even if you buy a picture/mirror box from a moving supply company, you will most likely have to cut and tape it to fit your specific piece. This is called "telescoping."

Furniture

Some furniture must come apart to move easily and prevent damage. Preassembled furniture should be disassembled for a move. If you break a joint on this type of furniture, it usually cannot be repaired. Remove the legs on furniture. This will save space and there will be less chance of damage to the item. Wrap furniture legs in bubble wrap or wrap old towels around them and bundle them with rope, twine, or packaging/mailing tape. Make sure that you put any nuts, bolts, and/or screws in a small, sealable plastic bag and tape the bag to the back of the furniture piece. The inside of an empty drawer is a great place to put very light, fragile items such as rolled posters or small lamp shades. You can leave your clothes in the drawers. However, the movers will merely place a "band" around the drawer to keep it from opening. Therefore, do not put anything expensive in a chest of drawers. Most movers request that the drawers, if someone else is moving your goods, not be too heavy.

Furniture with Glass Doors

China cabinets and entertainment centers must be taken apart when they are being moved. You can follow the wrapping technique in "Crating Items." Your goal is to secure the glass to a large, firm, flat, sturdy object and then cover it with thick cushioning, like a thick comforter. Then tightly secure the item with duct tape or rope. This should stand vertical and the mover should be aware that it is glass. If you are moving yourself, you should secure it vertically in the truck between two mattresses if possible. If the movers have to remove the glass and crate it, this will most likely increase your cost.

Sofas, Overstuffed Chairs

You can purchase "Stretch Wrap" from most moving companies for these items or use old sheets to cover them. Tape the sheet to the underneath of the chair/sofa. It could rain on moving day so protect your exposed furniture.

Lamps and Pillows

Most likely your lamps will be designated for a"last-minute box" because you will be using them until you move. Lamps should be taken apart and put into different boxes. The base should be wrapped with cushioning and put into a box with cushioning on the bottom. Put cushioning around it and on top of it. Pillows should be designated for the "last-minute boxes" as well because you will be using them until you move. Therefore, combining lamps and pillows in your "last-minute boxes" is a good idea. You can put other less fragile items in with a base of a lamp, such as well-wrapped 5x7 picture frames with glass or well-wrapped small vases or knickknacks. The shade does not need wrapped; however, you can cover it in plastic or put it into a large plastic bag and then box it the same as the base with cushioning on the top and bottom. Other extremely light and fragile items can go in with the shade.

Mattresses

Just like birthday parties, moving day always seems to be a rainy one! It is hard to find something big enough to cover a mattress. Moving companies can box or bag your mattresses. If you request this, make sure you know the cost and it is in writing in your contract before you move. You can also buy plastic wrap at a home improvement store to cover mattresses, or use old sheets and duct tape. It is a big chore to do on a busy morning. You can always wrap the mattress a couple of days ahead and then put a blanket over it and sleep on it. This way you will not have to wrap it the morning of move day. It is ideal to have your mattresses covered to protect them from dirt from other boxes, the truck, or the weather.

Rugs

Rugs are an easy item to forget about until all of the furniture is gone and then you realize that you want to take your area and throw rugs. Small throw rugs such as bathroom rugs make great cushioning for the bottom of a box that you put a fragile item in. For example, fold your bathroom rug and put it in the bottom of a box; now you can wrap any ceramic or glass decorations with bubble wrap or newspaper and put them on top. Remember a top cushion and mark fragile on the outside. I always washed small rugs after getting to my new place; however, it is a good idea to get larger rugs cleaned before moving and then roll them and wrap them in plastic. Once you get to your new place, you will not have to worry about finding a place to get the rugs cleaned.

Potted Plants

It may state in your moving company's information that they do not transport plants. However, you can ask the driver and he will most likely take the plants, but he will make you aware that there is no guarantee that they will not be damaged. Know the length of your drop-off window because if it is longer than five days, your plants may not survive. I recommend trimming plants prior to transportation so they will take up less space and there will be less chance of a branch getting broken off or damaged. I have drastically trimmed plants at the last minute so that they would fit in my vehicle. Then I would give them plant food upon arriving at the new place. I did overtrim once and the plant died, so be cautious. It is best to trim them a month before the move and give them some plant food so that they can recover from the trim by the time they need to be transported.

Outdoor Furniture

Folding chairs/tables should be folded, and the smaller pieces should be bound together, if possible, with twine or rope. Put your last name in very bold black letters on a piece of large paper and tape it to the furniture. Make sure that the movers mark them either by color or name so that they know that they are part of your shipment. Once the movers arrive at your new residence with your shipment, make sure that you remember the outdoor furniture. You can make a special Box Number Sheet just for the outdoor furniture even though it is not boxed. Outdoor furniture is an easy item to overlook and forget about when the movers bring all of your boxes and house furniture.

Lawn Equipment/ Outdoor Shed/ Garage

Shovels, rakes, and hoes can be bound together or bundled in a pad or old blanket. Drain the garden hose and coil and tie it. Try not to have very small bundles. Having a lot of small items and unboxed items makes it difficult to keep track of your inventory and increases the chance of losing items during the move especially if a moving company is taking your items.

Any tool that has a blade or sharp edge should be covered. You can fold a piece of thin cardboard around the blade and then secure tightly with tape to hold it together. Your garage contains a lot of items you will need to dispose of (see Hazardous List).

Clean Your Outdoor Items!

It is important to note that the U.S. Department of Agriculture enforces gypsy moth quarantine regulations requiring that your outdoor items be inspected for all gypsy moth life stages. This applies if you are moving from a state that is gypsy moth infested to a state that is not. You will most likely have to sign a form stating that you have inspected the outdoor articles that you are transporting. Your moving company should be able to provide more information on this matter. Pests on one item can crawl into boxes or furniture while on a moving truck.

Suitcases

If you are not using your suitcase as your Survival box, remember to pack it! I have actually completed packing and forgot that I could put items in my suitcases, and on moving day I was unloading a packed box to fill my empty suitcase! It is ideal to put your better clothing and accessories in your suitcases. Remember that most suitcases have locks, so you could put items in a suitcase that you are somewhat concerned about. You may want to purchase a better quality lock for extra security.

Transporting Firearms

The best way to transport your firearm(s) to another state is to take them to a firearm store in your current area and have them ship your firearm(s) to a firearms store in your new area. When you arrive, you can pick it up. However, if you will be traveling with your firearm(s), you must travel with it unloaded and have the firearm locked in a container and the ammunition in a separate package – it must be unloaded and not readily accessible. If you are traveling by vehicle, it is best to have these items in the trunk. If you are traveling by airplane, call the airlines or check the website for instructions. Do this for all the airports that you will pass through. Check their policy for transporting a firearm. State laws for handguns vary.

Survival Box

A "Survival box" is very important to make your time between homes comfortable. You may have several Survival boxes depending on how big your vehicle is. Suitcases are good to use for Survival box items, such as clothes, sheets, towels. You may have just one survival bag/suitcase if you are traveling by airplane to your new residence. Estimating how much you can take in your Survival box/bag can be tricky. You do not want to have too much to fit in your car or luggage after the movers leave. If you are traveling to your new home by airplane or train, you may not need as much. In this case, you may want to consider mailing boxes with necessities (for example, clothes you will need before the household goods arrive). You will need to have an address to mail the boxes to. Once, we mailed boxes to the maintenance office of the townhouse complex that we were moving to. The office held them for us until we arrived. Mail boxes a day or two before your flight. The boxes most likely will arrive before your household goods.

Survival Box List

Make a list of everything you want to take in the car/airplane especially if you are moving out of state or more than two hours away. If the movers give you a drop-off window, you should lean towards preparing for the later end of the window just to be safe. Your list should accommodate you for the longest possible window. The closer and closer it gets to moving day, the more and more it helps to have lists! Making this list early will help you avoid packing items that you may want to take with you in the car. I once packed some fragile items in a very solid and protective cooler we had and then realized on moving day that I needed that cooler for some food items that I had in our refrigerator and wanted to bring along. Coolers make a great container for transporting very fragile items; however, make sure that you will not need the cooler for food on move day. It is nice to be able to sit and have a drink and something to eat just after moving as you may not want to go to the grocery store right away.

Here is a list of items that you may want to put in your Survival box/suitcase (adjust to fit your specific needs):

air mattress	instant coffee or tea	sunglasses
aluminum foil	keys (car, suitcases, safe, etc.)	tape
aspirin	light bulbs	tape measure
baby items	make-up	telephone(s)
bath soap	medications/prescriptions	tool kit
bath towels	moist wipes	toothbrush
bed sheets	money/traveler's checks	toothpaste
blankets	muscle rub	towels/wash cloths
bottled water	napkins	trash bags
camera and film	night lights	travel alarm
can opener	paper cups/plates	video camera
change of clothes	paper and pens	Sealable plastic bags
children's games/toys/books	paper towels	
clock	payment for mover	_____
coffee cream	pet items	
coin/stamp collection	pet cage & food	_____
cooler	phone book from new city	
credit cards	phone book from old city	_____
currency	photo albums & videos	
deodorant	pillows	_____
dish soap	plastic utensils	
dish towel	scissors	_____
drinks	shampoo	
envelopes	shaver/shave bag	_____
expensive jewelry	silverware	
facial & toilet tissue	sleeping bags	_____
firearms	snacks	
fire extinguisher	sponges	_____
flash light	stamps	
food	sugar	_____

Do not forget your move folder with all of your important papers (move-related papers, automobile-ownership records, children's school records, medical and dental records, insurance policies, and address book)!

Note: If you have been living in a warm climate area and you are moving to an area where the climate is cooler, you will most likely need some warmer clothes in your survival box/suitcase. Make sure that you do not pack these items in boxes for the movers to take. The same applies if you are living in a cooler climate and you are moving to a warmer climate. If the movers tell you that your "drop-off window" could be 10 days, then be prepared for 10 days without your household goods! It will be nice if it is less, but you should be prepared for the longest period. You will not want to have to go to the store to buy clothes during that time.

Preparing Household Goods for Storage

If you will be leaving some or all of your household goods in storage for a period of time, here are some helpful tips.

- To avoid mice and pests, do not put food/liquids in storage.

- Use pallets underneath items to keep them off the floor, promote air circulation, and avoid damage if flooding occurs. Ask your local grocery or hardware stores if you can have their unused pallets. Make sure that you remove any nails to avoid accidents.

- Boxes should sit on plastic and be properly taped shut with mailing or packaging tape.

- Purchase an insurance plan for your stored items.

- Make sure you have a quality lock on your unit.

- If you are going to use moth balls, keep in mind that the "moth ball" smell is not easily removed from fabric. Sometimes dry cleaning cannot even remove the smell.

- It is not a good idea, for security reasons, to store valuables or important papers in a storage unit.

- Paintings/fine art, electronics, and musical instruments should not be stored in an uncontrolled-climate storage unit for an extended period of time.

- Washers and dryers must be disconnected and serviced. Hoses must be properly disconnected from the wall, drained, and sealed off with a plastic bag and rubber band. Secure spring-mounted motors by bracing the tub with special inserts that the moving companies have.

- Avoid using plastic on fabric furniture to prevent mildew. Instead use old blankets or sheets to cover furniture. Paper pads are also an option and are most likely available through your moving company.

- For clothing, seal them tightly in plastic bags to avoid picking up a permanent smell.

- Hazardous materials should not be stored in a storage unit.

- Any motorized item should have the gas tank drained and the gas cap loosely placed on the tank so it can breathe.

- Mattresses should be covered in mattress boxes or covered with blankets/sheets. Store a mattress on its side against a wall. A mattress can become "lumpy" if stored flat.

- A waterbed mattress should be completely drained. Contact the manufacturer to get additional information on how to preserve the mattress during storage.

- Clean the inside of all appliances with a solution of one cup of baking soda to one gallon of water. After cleaning, let the appliance door open for 24 hours so that it can dry completely to avoid mildew and odor.

- Store refrigerators and freezers with the doors slightly open. Place the electrical cord so that it hangs down from the top of appliance to keep the door from closing completely. However, you should prevent the appliance from being able to be opened completely to prevent a suffocation tragedy. Place charcoal briquettes on paper inside the appliance to absorb odors.

- Humidity can damage electronics that are stored in a non-climate-controlled storage facility. There are products available that absorb moisture in the air and help protect your belongings if you are using a storage unit that is not climate controlled. Check with your local hardware store to purchase these products.

Loading a Storage Unit

Once we moved to a temporary residence while we were looking for a permanent residence. The majority of our household goods were put into a garage. The boxes were all in the middle with furniture around them which left us without access to the boxes. For five months we had no access to our belongings unless we wanted to move all of the furniture. If you are storing your household items somewhere temporarily, this chart will can give you an idea of how to stack them so that you can have access to every box by just leaving an aisle on either side of the boxes.

Door to Storage				
BEDS	AISLE	BOXES	AISLE	COUCH
DRESSER				TABLES
		BOXES		
DESK				CHEST OF DRAWERS
LOVESEAT		BOXES		BEDS
FURNITURE				FURNITURE
ROLL OF CARPET		BOXES		LARGE APPLIANCES

Your mattresses and furniture should be stacked on both sides of the storage area tightly against the walls. Any crated items (mirrors, pictures) should be secure between the mattresses. Walking space should be left in front of the furniture (as a long skinny aisle). Boxes should be stacked, with the heaviest on the bottom, down the central part of the storage room with the numbers and writing (bedroom, kitchen, last minute, fragile) facing the aisles. You will be able to walk into the storage room and see all of your boxes. If you have a big storage area, you can create two aisles on either side. Fragile boxes can be stacked on top of the furniture. This a great way to arrange attics and storage rooms in your home.

If You Are Moving Overseas

When you have to ship your household goods overseas, they most likely will have to go through customs. You may have to become a resident before you can collect your household goods, and this can take awhile. You should try to pack as much as you can to take with you personally. You may want to purchase larger suitcases. Call the airline that you are flying with and ask what the weight and size requirements are. Customs will most likely open some of your household items. Some items may break or get lost during the process. If you are moving overseas temporarily, you may want to put some of your more valuable items in storage here in the United States or store items at a friend's or relative's home.

Tying Up Loose Ends

Pick up dry cleaning, layaways, and pictures. Cancel newspapers and put documentation of who you spoke to and the date in your move folder just in case the paper continues to be delivered to your old address at your expense. Return any library books or other items that you may have borrowed.

Banking/Extraordinary Value Items

You should keep your checking account and Certificates of Deposit active until after you move. Once you get to your new residence, you can open new accounts. You should close any safe-deposit boxes and keep those items with you when relocating. Consider getting traveler's checks/cards for your trip. All stocks, bonds, currency, stamps, coins, securities, jewelry, furs, insurance policies, and valuable papers should NOT be packed for transit in the moving truck. These items should be with you.

If your existing bank has a branch at your new location, I would recommend checking with the bank to see if you need new checks due to the bank having a different branch/region number of the checks. This could cause delays in simple transactions. You will need new checks with your current address. I would recommend closing and reopening any bank accounts.

Bugs Beware!

If you are moving to a warmer climate, you will definitely want to arrange for an exterminator to prepare your new house or apartment one week before you move in. If you move in and discover that you have critters, the exterminator will request that you clear your closets and cabinets so that they can spray. You do not want to move in and unpack only to have to move all the items out again.

Cleaning Service

After you or the movers have completely loaded your entire household of goods onto the moving truck, you may find that your empty home needs some cleaning. Once large furniture and appliances are moved, there can be dirt and even water underneath. If you rented a truck, you may be concerned about exceeding your time limit with the rental company and may not have time to clean. You may be exhausted and may not want to clean. One alternative is to plan ahead and hire a cleaning person or company to come in and clean your empty place. If you hire a cleaning company, you do not have to worry about leaving cleaning supplies or the vacuum behind. If your budget cannot afford a cleaning company, another option is for you to arrange for a friend or family member to help you or do the cleaning for you.

If you are going to do the cleaning yourself, you must remember to leave a vacuum cleaner, bucket, sponges, disinfectants, etc., in one spot and away from other items that the movers are taking. It can be very helpful to clean appliances, and possibly move large appliances and clean behind and underneath them a week before you move to limit your work on move day. If you live in an apartment your security deposit may not be returned to you if you leave the place unclean.

Transferring Medical Records

Call your doctor and dentist to find out if you can obtain a physical copy of your medical records. Explain that you do not have a doctor in your new area yet and would like to have the records in case something would happen while you are traveling to your new area. If you have to pay for the copies, I would recommend doing so just so you can have a hard copy for yourself. Medical centers sometimes remove old records and store them in another area if they have not seen you as a patient for a while, so do not prolong asking for the records that you need. Your current doctor may be able to assist you with finding a doctor in your new area. If you or anyone in your family takes a prescription medication, you can ask your doctor for a few extra refills to cover you until you find a doctor or pharmacy in your new area.

How Will "You and Your Family" Move?

Reservations. Once you figure out how you are going to move your household items and you begin packing, you must also consider how you, your family, and possibly your pets will move. How many cars do you have? Is there someone to drive each car? If you are driving, make sure you have your route mapped out. Will you be shipping a car? If you are traveling by airplane or train to your new residence, you will need to book reservations for traveling and for a hotel/motel if you need one.

Transporting a Car. If you are planning on towing a vehicle behind your vehicle or a moving truck, you will need to know the "towing capacity" of the lead vehicle. You will then need to know the weight of the vehicle that you are towing. It is important to get detailed instructions on how to use the transport trailer and how to properly secure the vehicle that you are towing. Auto transport trailers keep all wheels of the towed vehicle off the ground and can be ideal for long-distance moves. A tow dolly keeps the front wheels of the towed vehicle off the ground and is a great low-cost choice for front-wheel-drive cars. Motorcycle transport trailers are also available.

There are moving companies that can put your car right on the moving truck with your household goods! This is most likely more expensive than driving the car yourself; however, if you have two or three cars, it may be an option that you want to research.

Drive-Away Companies

A drive-away company helps you transport your vehicle to your new destination by finding people who will drive your car there. It is an interesting concept that is not well known. It is a lot less expensive than shipping a car to a destination. You can find these companies on the Internet by searching "drive-away companies." Contact the Better Business Bureau to make sure that the company that you choose does not have any complaints filed against them.

Important Tool Box

A general tool box (flat-and Phillips-head screwdrivers, drill set, crescent wrench, hammer, socket wrench) should go in the car with you. You will need tools when you are leaving your old residence and upon arriving at your new residence for taking apart furniture, dismounting a telephone, changing a lock, etc.

Car Maintenance and Tune-Up

If you are driving and following your household goods on a truck or meeting professional movers at your new location, you definitely want to make sure your car is in prime shape. If you are delayed or unable to meet the movers at the new destination, your household goods may be put into storage at your expense. Whether you are traveling alone or with your family, you should be concerned about breaking down in a remote area. It might be wise to join a 24-hour roadside-assistance program such as AAA.

Here is a list of items to check before taking your automobile on a trip:

- All interior and exterior lights
- Tires for wear and proper air pressure (buy new tires if necessary)
- Engine-oil fluid level
- Lap and shoulder belts for wear and proper function
- Air pressure in spare tire
- Power-steering fluid level
- Windshield-washer solvent fluid level
- Wiper operation (clean all wiper blades)
- Parking brake for proper operation
- Safety-warning lamps (brake, ABS, air bag, safety belt) for operation
- Cooling-system fluid level and coolant strength
- Battery connections (clean if necessary)
- Automatic-transmission fluid level
- Air filter (replace if needed)

Make sure you have these items readily accessible in your car:

- First-aid kit
- Aerosol tire inflator
- Flash light
- Fire extinguisher
- Cell phone
- Road maps and compass
- Driver's license
- Car registration
- Insurance identification cards
- An emergency kit (jack, lug wrench, flashlight, triangular reflectors or road flares, jumper cables, fire extinguisher, and salt or sand if you are driving in snow)

Note: For diesel, natural gas, propane, and hybrid vehicles check your owner's manual for additional checks and services. Also, check for special operating conditions such as:

- Towing or carrying a heavy load

- Driving in dusty conditions

- Extensive idling and/or driving at low-speeds for long distances

- Off-road operation

Your vehicle service center can assist you with further clarification on special driving conditions.

Registering Your Car

Car registration policies are not the same in every state. There are some states that base your registration fee on the value of your car. This can be quite a large sum of money! Make sure that you are aware of the registration policies prior to moving.

Contact the Department of Motor Vehicles (DMV) for the licensing center closest to your new zip code. At the DMV, you can change your license, title, and registration. However, if you are a member, AAA can also take care of these matters much more quickly than the DMV.

Note: If you have never moved, be aware that automotive policies and laws vary from state to state. Not all states require inspection, emission laws vary, etc.

Pay Up

If you have any unpaid tickets or taxes, get them paid before you leave. Unpaid tickets can result in a warrant for your arrest and/or suspension of your driver's license. It is easy to forget about a ticket and be surprised years later when it resurfaces if you are ever stopped again. You could be detained until you are able to resolve an unpaid fine.

Moving Your Pet(s)

Remember to get copies of your pet's medical records from the veterinarian before you move. You can also get a "pet sedative" from your veterinarian if you know that your pet may become distressed on moving day. Your pet should be fine while you are packing; however, he may panic, run away, or become ill on moving day when there is a lot of chaos. It is best to prevent him from seeing the movers take away your household goods. You will be very busy, and the last thing that you want to worry about is your pet getting stepped on, slipping out the door and getting lost because he is so scared, or hiding in a piece of furniture or box and ending up on the moving truck. Remember, your door will most likely be propped open for the movers, who are carrying the boxes and furniture to the truck. It is a good idea to designate a safe room to put your pet in while everything is being moved to the truck. You can use a bathroom that has been emptied out or even a large closet.

Before the moving truck arrives, put food, water and some favorite toys in this designated room for your pet. You may also want to put the pet's leash or carrying cage in this designated room since you will need it when it is time for you and your pet to leave. Remember to leave room in the car for the pet and/or pet cage. When the moving truck arrives and it is time to start loading, put your pet in this safe room and put a sign on the door saying "Pet inside—do not open." Your pet will feel much better inside this room. Make sure that you do not forget your pet when it is time for you to leave!

We always took our pets in the car with us after the movers left. The majority of the times we moved, it was over a five hour drive to our new residence. I had a midsize hatch-back which was filled with boxes of my most valuable items that I did not want to put on the moving truck. We would leave "cubby holes" between the boxes for my cats to hide in while we drove.

For long car trips, I recommend putting a piece of plastic down with a blanket on top for where the pet is going to be in the vehicle. If your cat or dog has an accident the plastic will protect your vehicle. One of my cats preferred to hide under my seat for the car ride. She did have an accident and the carpet under the seat smelled very bad. I put cat litter on the carpet under the seat for a few days and then vacuumed it and the smell dissipated. If you do not want your pet under your car seat, you can store an item there instead such as a blanket or a pile of magazines. Take bottled water and an empty water bowl so you can fill the bowl and give your pet a drink when you stop to rest. We traveled eight to ten hours sometimes, and I do not think the cats touched their food or water because they were so scared. Once we arrived at our new place, they quickly bounced back to normal in a week.

Once you arrive at your new place, you should immediately set up a designated "safe room" once again for your pet(s) before you take them out of the car. Put their food, water, and toys in the room and then bring them in. Shut the door until you unload the items that you brought with you. If you are bringing a lot of items in from your car, you will want your pet to be safe so they do not slip out the door and run away. After you have brought everything in, open the door so the animal can come out. The safe room is even more important when you are at your new home because if your pet slips out the door, he will not know where he is. Also, put the pet in the designated safe room again when the movers arrive with your household goods.

If you are driving over 10 hours to your new destination, you most likely will be staying overnight in a motel or with relatives or friends. Use the designated safe room for your pets in these situations as well. In a motel, use the bathroom as a safe room. If you are staying in a motel, ask for a ground floor room so you do not have to carry your pet up steps. You can search on the Internet for pet-friendly motels prior to moving.

If you are planning on moving your pet via airplane or train, be sure to call the airlines/train station well in advance to obtain the guidelines for transporting a pet. There may be an extra charge. You may need a certificate of health for your pet. Your pet will most likely need shots, paperwork and a certain kind of carrying cage. Some airlines have rules such as there can only be two dogs in the passenger cabin per flight. For this reason, you may want to book your flight reservations well in advance. If you are planning on transporting your pet below with the luggage, you should ask questions about air pressure and temperature in that area of the plane.

Partial Packing for Security

If you have hired a full service moving company to pack and transport your household goods, you may want to do some "partial packing" before the packers arrive. To eliminate the temptation of theft, especially with small, expensive items, you should prepack expensive clothes and accessories in a suitcase with a lock or in a box that is taped shut. Any expensive antiques or knickknacks should be packed in a box and taped shut prior to the moving company arriving.

Be aware that if you hire a full-service moving company, but pack some items yourself, the moving company will most likely not reimburse you if those items break during the move because they did not pack them. For this reason, pack with extreme care and use a lot of cushioning. Avoid having small, expensive items exposed when you have hired a company to pack your household goods.

The Day Before Moving Day

Ten Tips That Will Make Moving Day a Breeze!

Organization and preparation are key aspects of moving. Whether you have rented a moving truck or hired a moving company, these tips can save you time and money if they are done prior to moving day.

1. **Disassemble.** Make sure that all appliances are unplugged/hooked and "ready to go" and all electronics, entertainment centers, beds, and furniture are disassembled. Cover your mattresses. You can sleep on the covered mattress on the floor for one night.

2. **Communicate and Confirm.** If you have a babysitter and/or people coming to help on moving day, call them to be sure that they will be on time. Charge your cell phone.

3. **First Floor.** Move all of your household goods to the first floor. Bring items from the basement up to the first floor. Remove doors of tight doorways so furniture can fit through the door when the movers arrive. Keep your tool box close by.

4. **Organize.** Have all items that are going with you in an area where the movers will not accidentally take them. Review the Survival box list and make sure you have everything you need. Have fragile items, storage items, and last-minute boxes organized in separate places.

5. **Cleaning Supplies and Packing Supplies.** Set aside a cleaning-supply box, trash bags, vacuum cleaner, tape, and extra boxes.

6. **Say Goodbye.** You may want to visit your neighbors and say goodbye the night before you move because moving day is so very busy. If you are selling your home and it will be left vacant when you leave, make sure a relative, neighbor, or real estate agent has the keys and knows how to contact you. Also, notify the police department that the home will be vacant.

7. **Meals.** Make sandwiches and have drinks ready for moving day. If you will be traveling with a cooler, have it ready to go. Buy ice the night before and ask a neighbor to store it overnight for you if your freezer is unplugged. If you are going to order a pizza, make sure you have the number available.

8. **Gas and Money.** Make sure that all of the vehicles that will be traveling to your new home have a full tank of gas. Have cash and loose change in your car for tolls. If you are towing a vehicle, tolls may be higher. Make sure that you have the check or cash to pay the moving company.

9. **Return.** Drop off keys, garage door openers, computer modem, and cable box or any electronic equipment you are renting to their appropriate places .

10. **Weather.** If the predicted weather outlook is bad for moving day, purchase plastic to protect the carpet or use the "two carriers stay inside method" to prevent tracking mud, snow, or water into your residence (see Who's The Boss in the Moving Day section).

Loading a Truck

If possible, pick up your rental truck the night before you move to save time on moving day. Most rental truck companies have brochures or videos that give detailed instructions on how to load a shipment into a truck properly. I highly recommend making time to read or watch these instructions prior to moving. If you are loading your own van or SUV, make sure that you remove your spare tire and then load the tire last in case you blow a tire. You do not want to have to remove everything you have packed to get to your spare tire. If you have items that are going to storage, remember that you will want to load them on the truck last if you are going to your storage unit first and vice versa. This is a huge time and money saver on moving day. If you have pallets that you are going to put on the floor in your storage unit, you will want to load them very last because they will be the first item that goes into the storage unit.

The over-cab storage compartment in a moving truck is an ideal spot to store electronics, dishes, and fragile items. You may want to load these items first. Then load heavy items into the truck (for example, the stove, washing machine, refrigerator, and dishwasher). Load them against the far wall, close to the cab. Keep all appliances in their upright position or damage could occur. Balance the heavy items along the front and the sides.

Long items such as box springs, mattresses, headboards, sofas, and table tops should be against the walls of the truck. Face chest of drawers up against the truck walls or mattresses to prevent drawers from opening. Remember, each piece of furniture should have two- to three-inch-thick furniture pads or thick blankets to properly protect it. Tables should have legs removed; load the flat surface on edge (vertically). If you can not remove the legs, it should lay flat on padding or blanket with the legs up. Most moving companies can provide furniture padding if you do not have any. Disassemble bed frames and bind together. Sofas can be stood on end and anchored by other large items to save space. If mattresses and upholstered furniture are not covered, lift them up off the truck floor. Rolled carpets should be covered and placed on the floor along the side of the truck. Mirrors, pictures, and glass should stand up on edge between mattresses. Never lay pictures or mirrors flat. Mirrors and glass should stand on cardboard not the bare truck floor. The edges of boxes provide the most support, so when stacking boxes, stagger them the same way bricks are stacked. Heavy boxes should be low on the truck (bottom of the stack). Distribute heavy items evenly along the sides, down the middle, and front to back. Light boxes and loose items should be on top. If the vehicle has tie down rings to secure the load, use rope/straps to keep heavy items from shifting. A cargo net is best for full coverage to prevent items from shifting, although it may be hard to find. Fill any cavities with boxes to prevent shifting.

To prevent shifting, it is best if your truck is full. A half-full truck can be dangerous because your shipment can drastically shift. A half-full truck should be secured very well. Most moving rental-truck companies offer bracing materials that can be nailed to the wooden strips in the floor of the truck to help prevent shifting of your shipment. You can also use hooks and eyes to assist in tying down your shipment. It is a good idea to cover your shipment with plastic once it is loaded.

When you use a dolly/hand truck, you should pull it up the truck ramp or steps walking backwards for safety. Going down steps or a ramp, the dolly/hand truck should go down first. Always squat to lift boxes to avoid back injury. When you arrive at your destination, use caution when opening the door of the truck because items may have shifted and could fall out when you open the door, causing injury or breakage. Before leaving to transport your shipment, check all important aspects of the truck, such as the lights, breaks, turn signals, tires. If you are pulling a trailer, make sure you load heavier in the front. It is very important to have a fire extinguisher with you if you are driving a rental truck; make sure that you know where it is and that you have fast access to it in case you need it.

Easy–to–Forget Items:
- Dishes in the dishwasher
- Food and containers in the refrigerator
- Night lights and lamps
- Telephones, mobile phones, electronics
- Items hanging on the back of doors
- Items you may have put behind the furnace
- Items that you may have put on top of the refrigerator
- Items up on a bulkhead
- Item in the corners of your attic
- Window air-conditioning unit
- Outdoor items such as hoses, furniture, potted plants, and decorations (These items are easy to forget if you are moving in the winter.)

Permanent Fixtures

Remember, the movers who are coming to pick up your household goods do not remove any permanent fixtures such as mirrors, shelving, carpeting, electrical fixtures, drapery fixtures, or curtain rods. If you are planning on taking any of these items to your new place, you must have all of this taken care of prior to the movers arriving and you leaving or have special arrangements for the movers to take them but you will pay extra for this service.

Taping Boxes

As I mentioned in the Boxes section, I suggest taping the bottoms like those of packages you get in the mail. Do not "tuck" boxes shut. Over packing happens on move day, and those "tucks" can pop open easily. Fold in the short sides of a box first and then the long sides and run the tape from the top side of the box all the way down along the split and up to the other side of the box. Try to make sure the split in the box is in the middle of the tape strip. If it is going to be a heavy box, you may want to run tape across the other way on the bottom of the box as well. You can also tape the bottom inside of the box for extra support. If your boxes are taped well, they are secure.

I suggest taping boxes shut at least two days before you move because it is time consuming. You may run out of tape and have to go to the store for more. You do not want to be taping 40 boxes on moving day! Taping boxes shut early is good if you are well organized and know that you will not need anything from the boxes.

Moving Day

Communication

If you have an infant or a small child, it is wise to have someone there just to watch them so that you can properly communicate with the movers and they do not get in the way and possibly injured.

You should plan on being there before the movers arrive and while they are loading. They will have questions for you. They will want to know which items are going and which ones are staying. If you have boxes/items going to a storage facility, you should let the drivers know where these boxes are. They will want to either load these items first or last depending on when they are going to your new residence or to a storage facility. This should be in your contract prior to moving day. The movers may ask if there is adequate parking for their truck at the final destination where they will be unloading. They will want to know if they are unloading at an apartment or home and if it is a one or two story. Let the movers know if they will have trouble pulling up to your door at your new residence or if there may be cars in the way. If you are moving into an apartment and you suspect that other cars may need to be moved for the moving truck to get to your front door, you can give the movers your new landlord's phone number. Ask if the driver has a cell phone number that you can have.

It can be a big help to give the driver a printout of directions to your new home. You can include your new phone number and your cell phone number on the printout. Make sure your cell phone has been charged and that you give the driver the correct number. If you have any alternate numbers where you can be reached, give them to the driver just in case your cell phone does not work or is lost.

Organization

If you are really organized, you will have all of your boxes marked "Fragile" in one spot, all the boxes marked "Storage" in another (if your dropping anything at a storage unit), and your "last-minute" boxes further away from the others. Your Survival box/items that are going with you should be in a spot far away from the others so that they do not get carried off and put into the moving truck. You do not need to separate the boxes marked master bedroom, master bathroom, kids' bedroom, etc.; the movers will know how to arrange them. It is important for the movers to know where the storage boxes are because the movers will want to load them last so they can drop them off at the storage first. It is a good idea to separate the fragile boxes for the movers just so they can be extra careful with them and most likely load them on top of the heavy items. If you leave some fragile boxes open because you are waiting to top them with a pillow, make sure you do this before the movers arrive. Your pillows will be easy to find when you get to your new residence; just look for the "Fragile" and "last-minute" boxes! You can mark fragile boxes "this end up" as well.

Having your boxes organized is especially important if you are renting a truck because you will be on a time limit and being organized will help you avoid a late fee. Do not forget to list last-minute items going into last-minute boxes on the Box Number Sheets.

Who's the Boss!

Designate a coordinator to keep the loading process focused. If you are loading the moving truck yourself, have a meeting before the action begins. Sometimes when guys get together, the competition begins, and they like to see who can load the fastest and carry the biggest box! When this begins, they stop reading the boxes and paying attention to what they are doing! Let your help know that there is a strategy. Assign one or two people to stand in the truck and arrange the boxes on the truck. These people should have some knowledge of how to load a truck (see Loading a Truck). Assign the rest of your help to be carriers. The carriers and the helpers in the truck can switch jobs if someone gets tired, but the coordinator should stay the same. Let everyone know that the boxes are separated into groups: fragile, storage, and last minute. Tell them that the opened boxes are last-minute boxes and should be left until the end. (I actually had someone tucking my last-minute boxes shut and carrying them off!) Let them know which items are going in the car and show them where those items are. Inform your helpers that some boxes are marked "this end up" and that they need to read the boxes. The person standing in the truck should pay extra attention to what is written on the box. Everyone in the crew needs to know that the storage boxes must go on last so that they can be dropped off first. If you have bad weather on moving day, you can avoid tracking water, mud, or snow into your home by using the "two carriers stay inside method." Two men will stay inside carrying all items to the door where they will meet the outside help, who will carry the items to the moving truck. If you are unable to have one man stay inside, you can use carpet-protection plastic to protect your carpet. This plastic has a mild adhesive on the back to prevent it from sliding and someone falling. This plastic is not recommended for hardwood floors.

It is very important to maintain control on moving day. Cleaning behind a refrigerator, washer, or dryer can be done after the movers have loaded everything. Do not clean while the movers are carrying out your goods. You should be available to answer questions and make sure the correct boxes are being taken in the proper order. If you are following or leading the moving truck, the helpers will most likely appreciate a little break after loading. This will be a good time for you to clean. This is also a good time for a final walk through the house to make sure that no boxes were left behind. You will want to move in a timely manner, but you do not want to be in a hurry. Try not to have help that needs to leave at a certain time for another engagement. Find help that can commit the full day. Once we had planned on loading on Saturday and leaving on Sunday. Due to an approaching snow storm, we loaded on Saturday and left on Saturday.

Situations may arise that you have to quickly cram your move into a shorter amount of time. So, make sure your driver is OK with driving in all kinds of weather.

Once on the road, the driver should have a cell phone so she can communicate with the others. This is very important if there are people following the moving truck or vice versa.

Moving day can be overwhelming. If you have a moving company coming for your household goods, you can breathe a little easier. You will have done most of the work by packing, and the movers will shock you with their speed, professionalism, and efficiency. Make sure that children are out of the way for their own protection and to ensure that the movers will not trip over them. It is unnecessary to have family or friends help carry boxes out to a moving truck if there are professional movers there. Extra people helping can actually slow down the professional movers. Make sure that you are completely packed and have all of your boxes taped shut. The movers will not want to wait around for you to finish taping. When you are moving yourself, you have a little more time leaving those last-minute boxes open.

Delivery Day

Have your method of payment ready for the movers (cash, certified check, or traveler's check). If you are going to use a charge card, you will most likely need to have that approved one week or more before the movers take your household goods.

You will need to keep your inventory sheets and your personal Box Number Sheets with you. Do not feel rushed!!! It is very important to inspect all boxes for damage and make sure that all of your boxes are there. Be honest and inform the movers if you have any boxes that are not yours. If something is damaged or a box is missing, you should note this on the contract before you sign and you can put "pending" beside your signature. You may not want to sign if you have items missing. If something is missing or damaged, the driver may be able to give you a claim form immediately. You can fill it out and mail it right away. If the damage amount is quite large you may want to mail the form by certified mail. You may be so happy to be receiving your items that you may forget to check the inventory to make sure everything is there. We made this mistake once. Do not do this! Slow down and check!

You can file a complaint against a mover at www.protectyourmove.gov or by calling **1-888-DOT-SAFE (1-888-368-7238)**. In addition, you can file a complaint against the mover with the state attorney general and with consumer affairs agencies who investigate moving fraud.

Unpacking

Unpacking can be just as tiring as packing. First, you should set up the beds and then work on the kitchen. Look for those "Fragile" and "Last-Minute" boxes. If you have marked all of your boxes and numbered them, you should have no problem locating any items that you need. You can immediately organize the boxes into "open" and "put aside" sections in each room. It is wise to unwrap fragile items over a padded surface to avoid breakage. Be careful not to discard very small items or knickknacks that are wrapped in paper.

Some moving companies offer an "unpacking service" for an additional fee. This service consists of opening boxes, unwrapping items, placing them on a flat surface, and removing debris.

Moving Heavy Furniture

It is not a good idea to move heavy furniture by yourself. However, if you are attempting this, there is a way to move the object without rocking it or lifting it entirely. You can use a piece of cardboard or carpet to help slide the heavy object across the room. Place the piece of cardboard or carpet under one side of the furniture piece by lifting just that side. That one side should be totally on the carpet/cardboard and have no contact with the floor/carpet. Lift the opposite side and then push the object to slide it. Cardboard works best to slide furniture on carpet and a piece of carpet (carpet side down) works best to slide furniture on tile or hardwood floor.

Post Move

Make Sure You Are Receiving Important Mail

You may have to call creditors, car registration, license, primary care physician, etc., with your new address. Make sure you take care of transferring your driver's license, insurance, and registration. Pay any unpaid bills to previous utility companies.

Securing Your New Home

- Change locks

- Install dead bolts on doors

- Check and/or install smoke alarms/carbon monoxide monitors

- Buy fire extinguishers

- Install alarm/security system

Pets

- Find a veterinarian for your pet

- Get your pet a new license

New Stove/Appliances!

Take some time to get to know your new stove, appliances, furnace, fireplace, etc. I had a terrible accident with a new stove because I did not take the time to get familiar with the controls/burners.

Becoming a Resident

- To become a resident of a new state, the general steps are to live in the state, get a new driver's license and license plate

- If you will be going to college in your new town and are planning on receiving grants, you may have to become a legal resident by living there 1 to 3 years before you can receive the funds. Also, becoming a resident can lower tuition at some schools.

- If you have children who are going to attend school in your new town, you most likely will have to become a legal resident.

Possible Permanent Address

My husband and I had to move several times for his career to advance. We knew that the first three places that we moved to would not be permanent. Therefore, I used my parents address as a permanent address for very important issues such as 401k information and statements, investment statements, Social Security info, etc.

Telephone/Mobile phones

- Shop for the best long-distance telephone prices

- Most cell phone plans have free long distance

- Be absolutely sure before signing a contract with a mobile phone carrier. Speak to people in the area and inquire which company provides the best service/coverage. It can be very expensive to terminate a cellular phone contract.

Notify Friends and Relatives

It is nice to send your friends your new address via email, or if your move is near December, you can enclose your new address in a holiday greeting card.

Legal Services

Find a lawyer in your new area. Revise your will and other legal papers to avoid longer probate and higher legal fees.

Newcomers Club

Many towns have a Newcomers Club, which can be a nice way to meet new people and learn more about the town. When making new friends in a new town, it is a good idea not to complain about things that you are unhappy with and/or compare the new area with your old area. Nothing will push friends away from you faster!

Voter Registration

Register to vote in your new municipality.

Other Issues to Consider

Shop around for the best price for homeowners or renters insurance. Make sure you order new bank checks and return address labels as well.

The Emotional Side of Moving

"Don't Break the Chain"

When I was leaving my hometown for the first time, my dad could see how upset my mom and I were. He came up with the idea that if we continuously had arrangements to visit and we did not break the chain of visiting; we would always be looking forward to seeing each other. It really seemed to work well. Going back to my new home right after a visit with my parents was always hard, but soon after I would start getting excited to visit again!

Moving Away From Home – Ideas to help with the emotions of moving

What seems like just another day turns into an event that you never forget when you realize that you are moving. It has been said that moving is as stressful as marriage, death and divorce. When you find out you are moving and or have to tell a loved one that you are moving it is one of those moments in life that will visually stay with you forever. There are many different scenarios, you may be moving away from your family by yourself, you may be leaving with a partner and you are both leaving your family, or one of you may have family in the new town and one may not. In any of these scenarios it can be tough. College students are often leaving home and will not have family around them. So, how do you cope with the loneliness? I have a few suggestions.

My first move was to South Texas and I had two months from the time I made the decision to move until the time that I left. In those two months, I had to say goodbye to all of my family, pack, arrange and plan for my move. Those two months were not nearly as hard as arriving in Texas and being alone all day, when I was not job searching, and my fiancé was at work. After working for years and being surrounded by friends and family – this was a real mental challenge. Wages were very different there but I did finally accept a job and that was a life saver. Based on how depressing it was being alone for those two months, I knew that I needed a job." Working led to socializing and events that distracted me from missing my hometown. I was working in a 98% percent Hispanic environment and I am not Hispanic. My environment was very different for the first time in my life. You have to be a person who can jump on a new "band wagon" to have fun when you move. You don't have to stay on that wagon, but at least check it out or you may end up lonely and you will be without fond memories. You agreed to move because you are courageous, right? I decided to take an interest and learn about the Mexican food, culture and traditions and this kept me very busy and left me with a permanent love for some of the things I experienced and people that I met. When you show interest, new friends will be more willing to "show" and "invite" you to places. I went to Charro Bean festivals, local's parties on the island, folkloric dances, Rasta reggae parties, outdoor barbeque Christmas parties; I tried every Mexican dish available and took lots of pictures! It was all fun and made it easier to live there and the memories and photos still bring a smile to my face today.

I also lived in New York and made some big changes to adjust there as well. I was not a city driver before New York but if you want to survive in New York, you have to gain some courage and not think about it. Once you start driving in your new town, you can get around and that will keep you busy. I found and did everything that I could possibly do within my budget in New York, Connecticut and New Jersey to have fun and keep my mind off of being homesick. Visiting the surrounding towns will keep you busy and can be a lot of fun too. I made new friends once again in New York and tried to blend in and do what they were doing. If you reach out to people in your new town, you'll find some of them can be very nice and helpful. I had a Jewish friend who went to lunch with me to celebrate Easter because I was away from my family and alone on Easter Day. How sweet was that?

If you are a sports fan, take your team with you when you move but also try to show some appreciation for the new town's home team. It is easy to make friends when you have a common interest. I have to admit, as a die-hard Steeler fan, I once ate a piece of Dallas Cowboy cake at work, and wore a cheese-hat (Green Bay Packers) in a sports bar to be friendly to other transplants. I attended a Mets baseball playoff game party once as well. When people see you appreciating their interests then they may return the favor. I brought black and gold balloons and Steeler hats to my beach wedding in South Texas the day before the Super Bowl with Dallas vs. Pittsburgh. We ended up on the cover of the island's paper because of our originality. When people see you having fun, they will like you and want to join in. (That was the island, if we would have been in Dallas, it may have not been considered so cute to break out the black and gold that weekend.)

History may not be your favorite subject but I recommend visiting a town's historical sites while you are there. I toured the Alamo in South Texas, the Statue of Liberty and the Enterprise Carrier ship in New York and Valley Forge in Philadelphia. I saw the Liberty Bell and the national monument modeled on the picture of the soldiers raising the flag at the battle of Iwo Jima in South Texas (incredibly emotional to stand before). These are memorable things to do and see and the vision of them seems to stay with you for years. Try to acquire the desire to want to learn a little about the new town you are living in.

If you are a complainer, understand that complaining will not help. It will only drive new friends away from you and probably make your household unhappy if you have a partner and or children. Making negative comments in front of new friends about their town also is not helpful. Instead, try to solve the problem by being open-minded. Loneliness can be tough when you are living away from your family so try to stay connected with lots of pictures of them. Have a weekly scheduled video chat via Skype or Tango with family or friends. The lost art of mailing a letter (snail mail) is a good idea too. If you have a family member or friend living away from home send them a letter with a picture. They will really appreciate it. If you are living away from home, send your family or friends a letter with your favorite new restaurant menu inside or a newspaper article. They will like receiving something tangible from you. Always having arranged plans to see family and or friends is helpful and I call this "not breaking the chain" in my book the "Slick Move Guide". This may be hard financially if you are living far away, but even if the plans are in one year you may feel more connected. I was lucky enough to have a father who made sure that we never went past six months when I was living away from home. I flew home or my parents flew to wherever I was or we met somewhere in the middle for a vacation. This was helpful but someone needs to initiate the meetings. This is especially true if one partner has family locally and the other does not. This can cause a little tension so it is a good idea to invite the family that is not around to visit. There should be an effort by everyone involved to try and make reunions possible and harmonious. So, invite your family or friends to visit you and make an effort to return home once in a while. Keep in mind, if you and your partner are both away from family, remember, it may not be this way for long so enjoy the one on one alone time!

If you are complaining about the actual town, you need to realize that there are pros and cons about every town. If you concentrate on the cons, then you are not going to be happy. If you make up your mind to enjoy the pros and try some of the above advice, you may end of having a good time

Relocation and Keeping up Correspondence
I was in my twenties when I moved out of state for the first time. Being a little naïve, I left an unpaid phone bill thinking, "I'm out of here". Well, utility companies will have credit agencies hunt you down like a warrior. It is IMPERATIVE that you put forth an effort to change your address with all creditors and any organizations that you owe money to or your credit may be damaged. Family and friends will be less likely to hunt you down, and those are the people you would probably like to hear from, so it is important to inform them as well about your change of address. Here are some tips on how to change your address with creditors and also with friends:

Creditors: If you pay your bills online you may think there is no reason to change your home address, however, companies want updated information. Perks of having all of your information correct with online creditors are receiving coupons in the mail, having your credit report match and for online purchases your information will need to match.

If you pay your bills through the mail, you will need to change your address as mentioned earlier in this guide. This can be done via your post office by filling out a change of address form at the post office. You will need to provide a start date for when you want your mail to be stopped and all first class mail will be forwarded to your new address. You can change your mailing address online as well at **www.USPS.com. Tip:** It is also a good idea to speak with your mail carrier and let them know that you will no longer be living at this address after a certain date. Tip: For very important mail such as 401 K or any investment correspondence or any licenses that must be renewed yearly consider using a "permanent" address, such as your parents or a sibling if your move will be temporary. As important mail is forwarded to you, you can also change your address by using the change of address check box on your paper statement or by doing it online on their site. Keep in mind home owners, car insurance will need to be transferred or changed. Leaving a forwarding address with the previous providers is a good idea. You can change your address with the IRS at **www.IRS.gov** by downloading the appropriate forms. Refund checks are not always forwarded by the post office.

Family and friends - with so many ways to communicate today it's hard to believe that we fall out of touch with certain friends or relatives. Here are some tips to keep the flow of communication open:

If your mobile phone number is going to change most mobile phone providers can transfer your emails and contacts to your new phone. Send a text to all of your contacts notifying them that your number has changed. Some will save the new and delete the old, and some may not. For the ones who do not take note of the change try reminding them via e-mail of your new address and phone. If you send holiday cards, paper or electronic, include your new contact information. Tip: write your new address and new phone on the actual card. Return addresses on envelopes are often thrown away upon opening the card. If you are extremely organized, you can have address labels made and include one in the card so they can stick it in there address book or on a calendar. If after moving you feel that you have lost touch with family or friends, realize that you may have to be the initiator because many people may not be in the habit of reaching out to people who have moved away, "out of sight, out of mind". We tend to text, email and call people that we interact with daily. As the one who has chosen to move, you may have to accept more of the responsibility. Some friends/family may surprise you with a call or visit but the majority may need your initial effort to get them going. Keeping up communication can make family/friends seem not so far away.

Tip for mobile phones: Before switching a mobile phone carrier, research the new carrier for costs and length of contract and quality of service provided. The switch should be well planned to avoid getting locked into a carrier that is too expensive or provides a poor connection. Prior to switching make sure the new carrier can transfer all of your contacts and emails. Trying to get out of a mobile phone contract can be costly due to start-up fees and monthly charges not being reimbursed. Also you stand a chance of losing your phone number if you let time lapse 24- 48 hours in between switching carriers. Tip: If you are moving far away you will want to make sure that your new mobile phone provider offers a long distance calling plan.

Lastly – Don't forget about good old "snail mail", you may be surprised at how happy you can make someone by just sending them a letter; they will most likely want to respond. :)

 Eco-Friendly Moving Tip

LAST BUT NOT LEAST: If you think you might have to move again, SAVE YOUR PACKING SUPPLIES AND BOXES!! You can remove tape from boxes, flatten and bind them together so that they can be stored easily.

Moving Time Line

Prior to deciding to move, it is wise to make sure that you have fully investigated the area that you are planning on moving to. Make sure that you can afford to live in this area and that the area is able to meet your needs for living. Please see the first chapter of this book for investigating guidelines. Once you have investigated and you are satisfied with what you have found, it is time to set a move date and get busy!

Please note that everything in this time line is mentioned in this book. To fully benefit from this time line, you should read this book carefully. Not everything in this time line will apply to you, and you may have other particulars that are not included. Therefore, blank lines are provided so that you may customize this time line to fit your specific criteria. Also, this time line takes into consideration that you are working eight hours a day. Someone who is not working may have more time to pack and can wait a little longer to do these tasks listed on the following pages.

8 to 7 Weeks before You Move

- Take a trip to the area where you would like to move (see Investigate section!).

- Buy a move folder and notebook.

- Determine your move budget. If your company is handling the relocation, find out exactly what is covered and what you are responsible for. Once you determine your budget, you will have to decide how you will move.

- Consider truck rental, self-service move, or full-service move. Call moving companies and schedule at least three companies to give an estimate on what it would cost to ship your household goods. If you have already decided that you are moving yourself, research costs of truck rental companies.

- Make a list of questions for the moving companies that are giving you an estimate (see list of questions under self-service move).

- List your current house on the market as soon as possible or notify your landlord of your plans to move and provide an address for your security deposit to be mailed to you.

- Talk to real estate agents in your new area and let them know what you are looking for.

- Read moving-company and/or truck-rental-company policy and information.

- Have your expensive items appraised and take pictures of these items (antiques, jewelry, paintings, etc.).

- Locate storage facilities in your new neighborhood in case you have to put any or all of your household goods in storage.

- Locate important places in your new neighborhood, such as hospitals, medical centers, post offices, hotels, and motels.

- Begin donating, throwing away, selling, and sorting household goods (if you donate get a receipt for your taxes).

- Collect and buy packing materials (see list of things to buy and collect).

- Call the chamber of commerce in your new town and request a welcome packet; ask for answers to any questions that you may have.

_____

_____

6 Weeks before You Move

- Make a decision as to whether you will move by renting a truck, self-service move, or full-service move and if possible set a move date.

- Finalize contract with the movers and/or rental truck company. Let them know details like how much packing you plan on doing, if they will have to deliver to a one-story or two-story residence, if they will have to stop at a storage facility, etc.

- Pick up change of address forms at the post office.

- Make sure that you have the name of a post office in your new town and consider getting a P.O. box there if you have not found a new residence but you must move by a certain date.

- Consider what the climate will be like when you arrive at your new residence and make sure that you do not pack winter or summer clothes that you may need in your Survival box so that you do not have to purchase clothing upon arriving.

- Make a Survival box list so you do not pack any items that you think you might want to take with you in the car/plane.

- Purchase or collect moving boxes

- Empty a room for your "packed-boxes" room and move all packing supplies and empty boxes to that room.

- Set two or three empty boxes in each room with Box Number Sheets taped to each. With a large black marker, mark the box number on the side of the box to correlate with the Box Number Sheet that is taped to the box. Put a pen in each room so that you can write on the Box Number Sheet the names of the items that you are putting in the box as you pack.

- Begin packing (see Things to Pack First section) and move packed boxes into your packed-boxes room.

- Start eating frozen foods in your freezer.

- Decide how you and your family will travel to your new home and book flights, hotel arrangements, car shipping, rental car, etc., for move day.

- Decide how you will move your pet(s) and call the veterinarian if you need sedatives, a certificate of health, or shots

5 Weeks before You Move

- Arrange for a home inspector to inspect your new home if you have not done so already.

- Transfer medical, dental, and veterinarian records; cancel newspapers and magazines.

- Register children at new school and arrange to have records transferred. You may have to become a resident to do this.

- If you have any specialty items such as pool tables, hot tubs, or grandfather clocks, make calls and read owner's manuals to get specific transporting instructions.

- Put a bill/statement of every creditor you owe money to inside your move folder (charge cards, mortgage statement, doctors, dentists, newspapers, magazines, etc.) and remember to put any receipt related to the move in the move folder for tax purposes.

- Contact insurance company to make sure your belongings are covered during the move through your homeowners or renters policy. If not, find out how much the movers cover. Movers' basic insurance may cover items by the pound, which may not be enough; see what additional insurance the company offers.

- Contact friends/relatives that you would like to have help you move. Get them to mark their calendars!

- If you have small children, contact a friend/relative to babysit your little ones on move day. Make sure she marks her calendar!

- Arrange for a cleaning service to clean your old residence after you move or coordinate family or friends to help you clean after the place is empty on move day.

- Finalize travel arrangements, such as airline tickets and hotel reservations

- Continue packing

_____

_____

_____

_____

_____

4 Weeks before You Move

- You should have at least two rooms packed and empty (rooms that you do not use often).

- Take apart china cabinets and beds in guest rooms.

- Arrange for your utilities to be shut off at your current place and arrange for your new utilities to be turned on.

- Call creditors and give new address or do this online.

- Change your insurance policy on property, auto, and medical.

- Contact the Department of Motor Vehicles in your new area and inquire about forms that need to be filled out to change the license, title, and registration of your vehicle to your new area. Ask about the fees involved and if inspection and emission inspection are required.

- Get a P.O. box at a post office near where you are moving to if you have not yet found a residence but must move soon.

- Get a storage facility in your new area if you think you may need it.

- Begin packing items that you are not using in your garage, lawn storage shed, and attic.

- Eliminate hazardous and flammable materials from your household goods that you plan on shipping (see Hazardous Materials list).

- Arrange for an exterminator to examine your new residence before you move in

- Pay any unpaid tickets or citations you may have

- If you own a firearm, determine what method you will use to transport it. If moving to another state, you will have to determine if the gun needs a new registration and license.

_____

_____

_____

_____

_____

3 Weeks before You Move

- Confirm moving date with moving company, truck rental, babysitter, moving helpers, and any other arrangements that you have planned.

- Confirm delivery address, directions, and delivery date with the movers.

- Make sure that the change of address has gone through at the post office.

- Try to get the floor plan of your new place so you can determine where to have the movers put your furniture.

- Finalize insurance issues (homeowner's, car, protection plan for the moving truck).

- Trim plants back substantially; water them well so they recover from the trim before the movers arrive.

- Purchase a 24-hour roadside assistance program.

- Purchase an emergency kit for your vehicle

- Confirm your move in date with your new landlord, if applicable, and request a pest inspection.

- Purchase a general tool box if you do not have one.

- Remove pictures and decorations and mirrors from walls and pack or crate them.

_____

_____

_____

_____

_____

_____

_____

2 Weeks before You Move

- You should have four rooms packed.

- Finalize packing.

- Get your automobile a tune-up (see Tune-up list).

- If you are traveling by car to your new residence, you should have your route mapped out.

- If you are renting a truck, review tips on how to load a truck.

- Finalize your list of things that you will need in the car/plane with you (see Survival box list).

- Clean any carpets; roll and wrap them in plastic.

- Conclude financial matters relating to the sale or lease of your home.

- Confirm with family and friends that are helping for moving day (moving company, truck rental, and baby-sitter).

- Return library books or any borrowed items.

- Obtain pallets if you are putting items in storage.

_____

_____

_____

_____

_____

_____

_____

_____

1 Week before You Move

- Most of your home should be packed in boxes. Your attic and basement items should be packed, and those spaces should be empty. China cabinets and shelves should be empty and taken apart and crated. Items from the garage and shed should be packed and ready to go.

- Close safe deposit box; however, it may be wise to leave your checking account open if you have outstanding checks or automatic payments that have not been processed. You can close your old checking account from your new home via phone and send your signature via mail. Speak to a bank representative about any Certificates of Deposit that you may have and give them your new address so that when the investment matures, you can transfer it if necessary. Keep investment account numbers in your moving folder.

- Defrost freezer (allow 24 hours to dry) and clean refrigerator (if you are moving the refrigerator yourself, read the owner's manual for proper tie-down when transporting directions and make sure you have the proper tools to do this on moving day).

- Refill prescriptions and pick them up.

- Get traveler's checks/cards for trip or cash. Get cashier's check (method of payment) for movers.

- Drain oil and fuel from lawn mower, snow blower, and anything else motorized, and make sure that you will not be transporting anything containing hazardous chemicals.

- Return your gas grill's propane tank to the proper store.

- Properly cover any sharp blades on lawn equipment and gardening tools.

- Arrange for the moving van to be able to park as close as possible to the door of your new residence to avoid extra costs for a "long carry."

- Figure out a simple meal plan for the next week. Decide what and where you will eat the night before the move and the day of the move. Have delivery phone numbers posted on the door or refrigerator. Buy only the food that you need for the next few days.

- Get paper plates, cups, napkins, and utensils.

- Give a close friend or relative your travel route and schedule and keep a copy for yourself.

- Start packing your Survival box with critical items (see Survival box list) and put this box in a corner with other items that you will be taking in the car/plane with you. Make sure this box and other items are away from items the movers will be taking. The box should be marked "Do not move."

- If you are moving to an apartment and there is a chance that there may be other tenants' cars in the way of the moving van, call the landlord and ask him to let other tenants know that they may have to move their cars on moving day.

A few days before you move

- You should have a plan for how you will cover your mattress and, if possible, you should cover it and sleep on top of the cover. The less big tasks that you have to do in the next couple of days, the better.

- Disconnect electronics, computer, and entertainment centers.

- If you have told the movers that they would not have to go upstairs, make sure that all of your boxes and furniture are on the first floor. Push furniture aside to make room if you have to.

- Set aside a cleaning-supply box and vacuum cleaner if you are not having a cleaning service do a postmove clean on your current residence.

- Make sure that you have your move folder in a safe spot where you will not accidentally pack it. Make sure that it contains all the vital documents and information: contracts, bill of lading, rental policies, financial papers, new keys, maps, passport, and traveler's checks (unless they are in your purse or wallet).

- Make sure that you have all of your medicines packed in a leak-proof container so that you can carry them with you. Also make sure that they do not get packed on the moving truck.

- If you will be moving your washer and dryer, you will want to wash all the clothes that you will need for the trip and pack any dirty clothes from your laundry room.

- If you are moving your washer and dryer, you will want to disconnect them and get them ready for transport (read the owner's manual on transporting or call the manufacturer).

- If the predicted weather is looking bad for moving day, purchase plastic to protect the carpet or use the two carriers inside/two carriers outside method to prevent tracking mud, snow, or water into your residence.

- Drain your garden hose and roll it up to be packed.

- Visit with loved ones that you will be leaving behind. You may not have time for this on moving day.

- Purchase/Print a map in case GPS fails.

- Return cable equipment or any rented electronics/modems.

- If you told the movers they would not have to go to upstairs, make sure everything is on the first floor.

1 day before you move

- If you are renting a moving truck, you may be able to pick up the vehicle the night before.

- If your home will be left vacant when you leave, make sure a relative, neighbor, or real estate agent has the keys and knows how to contact you. Also, notify your insurance agent and police department that the home will be vacant.

- Double check closets, drawers, shelves, attic, basement, and garage one last time for items that you may have forgotten.

- Double check your meal plan for tomorrow and make sure that you have all of the groceries that you need. Have numbers handy for ordering food. If you are going to offer the movers' lunch, have the food and drinks ready.

- Take a walk outside of your residence to see if you may have forgotten to pack any toys, lawn furniture, decorations, etc.

- Do not forget to buy ice if you are traveling with a cooler.

- Have the cashier's check/method of payment and the tip (if you are tipping the movers) in a place where you can access it easily (move folder).

- Make sure that your refrigerator is clean and that only the food that you plan on taking and eating tomorrow is inside. Making sandwiches and packing snacks the night before is helpful.

- Check your tape, trash-bag, and empty-box supply. It is good to have a few extra boxes on moving day for any last-minute items that you may have forgotten to pack.

- Charge your cellular device(s)!

- Make sure that all vehicles that will be traveling to your new destination have a full tank of gas.

- Make sure that you have money for toll booths for all of your vehicles.

- Pick up storage unit keys.

_____

_____

_____

_____

_____

Moving Day

- If you are picking up a rental truck, inspect the truck before driving it off the lot (see Deciding How You Are Going To Move)

- If you are renting a dolly from a moving or truck rental company, don't forget to pick it up.

- Have a brief meeting with your helpers (see the previous Moving Day section in this guide).

- See the Items Easy to Forget list in this guide.

- Remember to leave your keys, garage door openers, and forwarding address with the new responsible party.

- Close and lock all windows and doors.

- Set temperature and turn all appliances off before leaving and shut off water.

- Make sure the refrigerator, dishwasher, and oven are empty.

- Unplug and pack all phones.

- Discuss the drop-off window with the driver and ask if you can have the driver's cell phone number and confirm delivery address.

- Give the driver your cell phone number and directions to your new place. Give him any important instructions about the location of the new residence, and make him aware of any difficulties with pulling in front of the new residence to unload.

- Drop off cable box/computer modem if you have not done so already.

- Don't forget to leave your forwarding address with your landlord if you are expecting a security deposit refund.

For your convenience, I have provided a Box Number Sheet for you to make copies for all of your boxes so that you can have your own detailed inventory after you have completed all of your packing. See the Smart Packing Section for more detail.

1. _____
2. _____
3. _____
4. _____
5. _____
6. _____
7. _____
8. _____
9. _____
10. _____
11. _____
12. _____
13. _____
14. _____
15. _____
16. _____
17. _____
18. _____
19. _____
20. _____

21. _____
22. _____
23. _____
24. _____
25. _____
26. _____
27. _____
28. _____
29. _____
30. _____
31. _____
32. _____
33. _____
34. _____
35. _____
36. _____
37 _____
38. _____
39. _____
40. _____